LAWRENCE GOWING

Lucian Freud

THAMES AND HUDSON

The publishers gratefully acknowledge the assistance
given by James Kirkman, the artist's agent.

First published in the USA in 1982 by Thames and
Hudson Inc., 500 Fifth Avenue, New York, NY 10110

First paperback edition 1984

Library of Congress Catalog Card Number 82–80250

Printed and bound in the Netherlands

At the outset there is always a mystery. We cannot know what a painter brought to painting or what drew him to it. Yet everything he paints throughout his life adds to our understanding of one or both these things. When his last picture is painted in that predestined way in which, one cannot help believing, an artist's work, and therefore *art*, unfolds – when the last predestined picture is finished and the trajectory of his meaning completes its curve – then we know all there is to be known about these first riddles and understand what can't be known, what remains unknowable about the sources and the resources of a painter.

This book offers a chance to look at work by Lucian Freud. Generally the sight is not easy to come by, because most of the pictures belong to people, not museums. It is nearly ten years since as many of them as this were shown together. Unlike most noted contemporaries, Freud does not paint museum pictures, though if you come on one in a museum you may never forget it. Large groups of them hang in a few collections; his pictures are sought after and kept at home, as if there was something personal in their significance. This book, in which Freud has taken a large part, is exceptional in another respect. Not only the work but the view of it here (though not the commentary) is his own. Seen through his eyes, the pictures show aspects that are unexpected. In his comparisons, cutting sometimes a little across the order in which they may have been painted, they connect in ways that one had not foreseen. Seen in his context they show more of ... something or other, which one had not noticed, more of a character that is peculiarly his. They not only complement each other; they reveal more of the unpredicted discords that are an elusive element in them. Led by the painter, one is aware at page after page of a residual shock from which familiarity does not shield one. One would not wish that it should. One rather, and shamelessly, prizes the frisson, without particular sentiment for whomever, in what unsparing involvement, inspired it. Familiarity does not shield but sharpens, engaging one more deeply in a relationship that is addictive.

With modern art in particular one is always considering, or should be if one is not, the shades of indispensability that attach to the surprise. The way that Lucian Freud's world presents itself to him and to us has been inseparable from a chill of incongruity that preserves its particularity, its otherness, as if a coldness in the figurative substance made the visual contact electric and compelling.

There is always something more or less unexpected in the unfolding of an original artist's work; because few of such people exist at one time we remain unaccustomed to the fact. One is never prepared for the edgy, restless mobility that continually implies something more and different until the artist's last picture has been painted. As I write Freud has just passed his fifty-ninth birthday; this concluding and conclusive evidence is a long way off. The latest picture on his easel is as full as any of the peculiar personal momentum that one has known from the beginning, but in every other respect so different that I find myself understanding afresh and differently a condition of private liveliness that was already apparent when I became aware of him more than forty years ago. Apparent and slightly irksome; I was inclined to resent it, and was lately concerned to find that Freud regarded this evidently unconcealed inclination of mine as a positive qualification for writing about him. I first knew this quality of liveliness, for which I should prefer a word that did not suggest animation or wholesomeness, when I think as much of a coiled vigilance and a sharpness in which one could imagine venom (my critical equipment was primitive and my sympathies limited) – knew it as a quality of drawing, one that was intrinsic to line and indeed to edges. Freud's view of a subject was marked from the first by a serpentine litheness in the ready, rapid way in which an object was confronted, the object of intellectual curiosity or sociable advantage or desire – it was apt then to be all of them at once. A personal flavour that was unlike any one had known was communicating itself to art; it still does. Going to look at the heads in the new picture, I become aware that this uncommon condition is now a condition of the paint, of the material itself and the incomparable alertness with which it is moulded to the experience of people. In the paint itself, through its receptive granulation – and equally through its miraculous lack of anything like the approximating mellowness that one had thought endemic to malerisch figuration, one feels the quality of sharpened perception and pointed response that makes one think of the lowered muzzle of some hunting creature, and think with involuntary admiration, unless it is apprehension.

One may recognize the latest work and the earliest, as well as the successive styles between, as one man's uses for art. That is not to account for them. Painting offers itself unaccounted for, uninterpreted, unexcused. Freud's rather few remarks about art in general set store by the defiantly inexplicable spell that the image arts achieve at their peak. The viable, sure-footed, impenetrability of his persona is intended. Again, one is now unaccustomed to a daemon like this in the polite community of the visual arts, but in the past art was full of such people. This is how the young men of the Renaissance must have been, with their eyes on anatomy and the main chance, on the street corners at evening when the botteghe came out and the virgins were hurried indoors. I have been able to confirm rather few even of the relevant details of Lucian Freud's childhood and how he came to painting. There is no evidence for most of the circumstances, least of all the highly coloured ones, that have been described. These myths were not Lucian's myths.

The undoubted facts are far enough from the usual experience of English painters. Berlin in the twenties was quite unlike a settled English nursery. Lucian's father, an architect, was the youngest son of Sigmund Freud and Lucian was born in 1922, in December, a month that is prolific in painters; one becomes accustomed to finding that they were a year younger than one had supposed from their dates. The cultivated household was hung with Hokusai prints and suchlike things, like a household anywhere, but there was an awareness of Vienna – the style, the probing and the abandonment. Lucian's grandfather gave him prints of the *Seasons* by Bruegel. In a Viennese climate rather than a German one, a special perceptiveness was natural to him and still is. The Austrians are conscious of a ludicrousness in the German language and when the subject of privacy comes up, Freud thinks of one of the *Gallows Songs* of Christian von Morgenstern, a quatrain in which the poet advises that the fidgety molecules of the flesh be left to chase each other and the ecstasies held sacred; a good edition of the *Gallows Songs* comes quickly to Freud's hand. He remembers nothing of his mother's family estate near Kotbus except the rampaging of the horses when the stables burned down. The only effect of the Reichstag fire was that in order not to be made aware of it the pupils of the Französisches Gymnasium took a roundabout way to school. Beach life on a Baltic island in summer left the well-cared for boy equally unaffected. There is not a shadow of C.D. Friedrich anywhere in his background or foreground to this day, any more than there is of Gerhart Hauptmann. That is all and more than all there is to say. We know nothing of how it was that by 1933, when the family moved to Britain, Lucian was drawing all the time.

Among the plates in this book, where Freud reveals as much of himself biographically as he 2 is likely ever to want or need to, the grazing sandstone *Horse* which occupies the first of them, it seems unrevealingly, backs into prominence quite oblivious of standing for a sense of animal community, which Lucian already felt at school in England, where he took riding instead of art. At school he carved the three-legged beast – the bent hind-leg stands for two – cropping patiently with a horsey delicacy only visible in the oriental curves of eye and muzzle, which are seen in a photograph that is not illustrated here – rather deliberately hidden, as if the linear chiselling would betray something earnest and unbecomingly naïve in such a prominent place. There is nothing for it but to back into prominence, animal-like and inarticulate. Yet that is revealing; in a year or two when Freud draws a man holding a pigeon, one has a sense of man and animal together, which occurred to one or two of the painters who were Freud's contemporaries and friends. Yet when he returned to it, it was very much Freud's own, and remains so – offensively for those who think it beastly of the naked boy, whom he painted forty years later, to be fondling a rat with whatever affection in flamboyant proximity to his genitals. The nearness is permitted by trust in the naturalness of the relationship. The community, which is also genital community, is always present just under the surface of this view of living things. At school Freud painted in the oil painting club; we also hear of him in the recollections of another good painter as a member, with goodness knows what other talents, of the backward Latin class. When he left, as he did leave schools, in a hurry, he abandoned his clothes and packed the sculpture.

In London, his father took the stone horse to the Central School of Arts and Crafts. Due to the horse, Freud supposes, he got in; there would not have been much doubt. People who met Freud in his middle teens, and a lot of people did, recognized his force immediately; fly, perceptive, lithe, with a hint of menace. I met him first in the winter of 1938–39 when he was

fifteen or sixteen and already spoken of as a boy-wonder. He was in a studio flat in Charlotte Street, round the corner from the house where Rimbaud and Verlaine took rooms, in company with a self-appointed Svengali who showed him off, whispering behind his hand, 'Marvellous!' Someone had made a trail of elfin footprints across the floor, up the wall, along the ceiling and out of the window. The great Surrealist exhibition in London was only just over; the strong impression was the disjunct and matted detail in Freud's drawings of the time – in which I recognized a kinship to Dürer that I was averse to, infected as I was with French flu and Bloomsbury snobberies. Any sign of the Teutonic was to be met with the mood of superiority in which Helen Anrep (living four doors up the street) had toured the galleries of Germany with Roger Fry. 'Poor dears', she said, 'We had to explain to them that Dürer

simply didn't exist.' So the pointed intensity apparent even in Freud's juvenile vision got under the English guard. It was a wounding penetration by something that didn't exist, and in combination with its beauty, as well as his beauty, it was irresistible. At the first night of a Sean O'Casey play, for which I had painted a big cloth of an evening sky, I discovered the sharpness of his insight when he added to Stephen Spender's compliments the rider, 'Except the second patch of blue'. He had spotted the extraneous sentiment unerringly.

Remembered, England at that moment – Munich England – seems to have been frightened yet also inert. One thinks of Freud's snaky acuteness flickering through it. Chiefly he was drawing then, with the sharp literalness which seemed naïvely to defy expectations from art. The defiance, and the drawings too, were real enough. They showed no awareness of the conventional distaste for categorical, German-looking detail – the most unfashionable look in art. Painting presented itself as drawing to Freud, because any other medium seemed beyond him. He thought the qualities that he admired in painting were too far removed for them ever to bear fruit for him. For a start, the quality produced by people who were steeped in painting was to be avoided at all costs. Appreciations of colour, for example, only meant that a picture did not work. People used the word 'colouring', which seemed to him particularly damning. Freud wanted colour to be the colour of life; it would not be thought of as colour, but as content. He dreaded the dreary look of paint as everyone else used it.

The pictures that stayed in his head were the things that disturbed him – things that were soothing had much less quality. And what were they, these disturbing things? He remembers Soutine's dead animals and Huysmans' book on Grünewald, which he still keeps by him – drawing again. Drawing, in fact, was a defence against the received idea of painting. If he felt that drawing was easier for him, it was not because he had any facility. But he believed that if he concentrated enough, he would draw well. None of that effort seemed to help him in painting. It was a long time before he felt the slightest freedom to do things in one way rather than another. For him there were no two ways about it; it was a matter of necessity – 'just as people are necessarily fond of their children'. With his lack of control, he felt that painting would be laboured.

It seems that at this moment he had no guiding conception of painting except that it would be lifelike and unlike any existing painting. A prototype would have been no use to Freud. 'My method was so arduous', he remembers, 'that there was no room for influence.' Freud moved easily in bohemian London. He took friends from school in lordly fashion to the Café Royal, for which he had a passion. He was a spectator of refugee society, and two or three years later he painted *The refugees*, embodying acute and sympathetic, though discrepant observation. A *6* man in dark glasses in the centre was a dentist in the Finchley Road until a year or two ago.

These first figure pictures were remembered or invented or imagined. They are thus quite different from the painting of people which has occupied Lucian Freud ever since. The later pictures are painted in the presence of the subject and all of them depend directly on information that is observed, information of the most specific kind. The invented and remembered pictures painted before he was twenty reflect an altogether different habit of thought – an imaginative drift, a reverie, a daydream of the actual, which is also in general

specific, never vague or capricious. What we watch is the actual stream of invention, the re-imagining rather than a process of observation. A current ripples across the picture; the surface is streaked and marbled by the imagining, as water carves ripples in the sand. These ripples do not model actual form; they recreate the general undulation of relief and a variation of imagined colour which is like a reference to the passage of light. I am aware of this first in
8   *Landscape with birds*, with a boy, skipping along – the only entirely carefree and arbitrary imagining anywhere in Freud's work – outlined against the bright iridescent distance, which is also a province of the sky, filling the top of the picture. *Landscape with birds* was dreamt with the visionary distinctness of childhood. Feathers and twigs divide like fan-shaped splinters in the pearly light of an immense panorama which is as much like furrowed cloud as hilly landscape.

Look as closely and as sceptically as you will, the innocence rings entirely true. If it seems improbable that Freud at eighteen, with such cultivated contacts, should still have been free from artfulness, the answer is that both alternatives could be true. Such a talent is likely to include the ability and the intention to preserve more from childhood than most have the wit to. The patterns of imagining here, both the fan-shaped splintering and the diffuse undulation that makes visible the process of imagining, remained with Freud for several years, giving shape to more specific things. The frontier of adulthood and the criteria of innocence, indeed the idea of maturity itself, are all different for a temperament like this. In *The refugees*   *6* the dentist's sunken cheeks and sloping forehead are creased with melancholy, as if washed and channelled by the flow of sympathetic insight. In the self portrait, which has been said to   *II* date from 1939, though it was conceivably painted later, the stream of imagining has passed

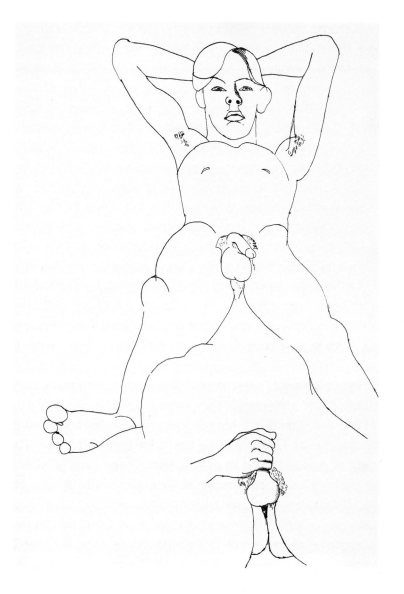

repeatedly to and fro across the head, leaving scarves of deeper colour, streaked with brown and crimson-pink, flattening the relief a little, yet depositing the substance out of which nose and lips materialize like sand-banks in the current. The drawing is half dissolved or washed outwards towards the edges of the little canvas, where the contour is entrenched or defended like identity itself. But the vestiges are exquisite and precious – little hedges of eyebrow over the attenuated almond eyes, pale and shallow; lips and nostrils which are rounded with smooth perfection in the reflected light. Within the whorls of an ear and around the jaw, the contours are none the less decisively mapped. Again, we are in doubt about the frontier between what was naïve, deliberate, guided or instinctive. The canvas is so fulfilled that one cannot believe that anything was frustrated. Just these questions must have been the subject of the boy's dialogue with himself. Woolly tie and hair and his green surroundings knit him about; within them the embodiment materializes. We watch the boy visualize himself.

These pictures conceive the real from a certain distance. What is remarkable is that we are watching develop the capacities to envisage and to embody, which eventually equipped one of the great literal, outward-looking artists of the century. He is teaching himself to dream a dream of the real, to dream from nature.

Perhaps the most remarkable of these juvenilia is a reverie about reverie. It developed out of a time in hospital. A little nurse and tiny patients, vanishing into the distance, establish the locale. But in the foreground of the *Hospital ward*, the figure lying in bed, playing the part that *23* was in fact the artist's own, was based on a daydream of his friend Peter Watson. The rhythmic weave of imagining passes again across and across; out of the creased pillow, with the sense of lonely affliction, drawing the feeling face, weaving the shadowed features, almond-shaped in the oval head. If one liked Peter Watson, as I did, it is an enchanting reminder, with just the graceful, yet brooding presence of the man. Of course a good painter is inexplicable and we do not know how anyone can nourish observation by indulging a faculty that is apparently just the opposite. Lucian Freud can and did. Sharing his dream of the real, we feel that the skipping, prancing boy in *Landscape with birds* is absolutely genuine and *8* justified in boasting, as it seems, of what is instinctive to him. There in the bright, channelled landscape of fancy, with the whole real, physical world before him, he has something to boast about.

From Regent Street someone took Freud to a famously raffish café in the streets off Charing Cross Road. There a friendly girl dispelled his illusions about the centrality of the art school that he was attending and told him that *the only place* was the East Anglian School of Drawing and Painting, which Cedric Morris ran at Dedham. There he went in 1939, feeling that here was an actual painter, by no means unapproachable, and filled by the glamour of it. Morris's way with paint banished the spectre of the laboured picture. He painted as if he was unrolling a scroll, confidently finishing each strip as he went. Freud painted the creative malevolence of the man with some of his own summary confidence and an intensity that never *7* got into Morris's pictures, unless it was those nearest to caricature. Morris was moody and prone to violent rages and he was considerably tried. Smoking at night, Freud accidentally burned the school down. But he was able to stay on with Morris, who allowed him to work at his own home, and paint flower pots and cactuses in the stable at Langham. The box of *3* apples, Freud's other approach to the painterly substance that he had been avoiding, was painted in the same place; the mountains were added later in Wales. In 1942 he smuggled *5* himself into the Merchant Navy. At sea he drew the amiable gunner stationed to defend his *22* ship. A girl he rather liked at Morris's school, whom he thought of as the girl he left behind him, was the subject of a maritime portrait on the quayside. In a few months he was invalided *28* out. A time in hospital that followed was recalled in his moving picture of the place.

The waterlily, like an imaginary bibelot, assembled with the memory of a precious friend on the hospital bed, introduces us to a continuing element in Freud's pictorial behaviour, the modus vivendi that he was growing into during these years. For him painting has to be, among other things, the collection of objects that he likes, the realizing of data that he values, an accumulation of what he enjoys or desires – it amounts to the same. It amounts to the compulsive necessity to be no one – not the gay show-off, poetic wonderboy, café-society seducer – no one and nothing except his own kind of painter, the ungovernably greedy, human kind. The treasures that he began in these years to incorporate in painting could be the amenities of his own life or the fate of some beautiful animal, the parts of an inviting body or the features that are each an earnest of some craved and intimate rapport. The details were on the surface miscellaneous, discrepant. On another level they are none the less homogeneous and consistent. They own a common motivation, which is the serious reason for representing anything and the only incentive to attain the quality that gives the contents of painting the value that they have in life. Painting for him has the character of his appetite, the preternaturally sharp-eyed appreciation, which is also a kind of possessiveness.

Cedric Morris had moved to Hadley. In convalescence Freud went back to work there.

8 Within a couple of years of the clear innocence of *Landscape with birds*, but with much experience behind him, he was painting and drawing the village boys who came to pose at Hadley with a clarity of an altogether different kind, the clarity of perception, which has remained at the heart of all his work. Yet at this stage Freud's assessment of what is seen was realistic only in the sense that a balance sheet is realistic. He was drawing such figures from

17 life, with literal, scratchy faithfulness, and also from memory, out of his head, with the bulging

16 vitality of graffiti. The only thing he had no sense of was the convention that objectivity

9 resided in a measured zone of emotional neutrality. When he came to paint the boys, there was no pretence that his eye was disinterested. Each model was rendered on a scale proportionate to his interest for the painter (Cézanne twice failed the test for the Ecole des Beaux Arts because of 'an excessive sincerity . . . a head interested me, so I made it too big.') With Freud, a boy in the centre, made fascinating by his brooding resentment, was painted half as large again as the pale and patient mother's boy beside him; two shadowed, watching eyes, recognizable as the artist, are buried in the background. A muscle-bound pin-up, in a sheet of drawings pinned on the easel behind, completes the range of the assortment.

Freud's exploratory approach in these first pictures was undeterred by the limits of his capability. He remembers that he was still unsure whether paint was in his power to control. Control was indispensable; he returns to the word again and again in describing how he began. If anyone was to be swept away, it would not be him. If any picture was to be laboured, it would not be his. One would guess that the object of his extraordinary concentration in these years, when he left aside anything over which he could not exert a kind of mastery, was exactly this control, dominating like a tyrant the attractive subject and the refractory medium alike.

The control in the drawings at Hadley is the rigid dominion of modern classicism. It could only be the ideal of someone who had grown up an heir to the confident clearsightedness and the ironic traditionalism of advanced international taste in the 1920s, in which disruption, fragmentation and distortion were assumed; they were no longer frightening; they were in the past. It remained to dominate them and use them to rule anything that could be anarchic or

12, 13, disobedient in the human subject. Freud's drawings in 1943 and 1944 have already a quality

14, 15 of resolved classical line, with the minimum of inflexions to make legible its formal message,

which is otherwise the property only of the very best painters of twenty years before. This is a language which Freud spoke by nature and upbringing, yet had to repeat over and over until it carried a tone of command, a peremptory note almost of injunction to his model, or a merciless reference to the fate of disjected heaps of fur and feather in still-life.

Style and capacity developed rapidly in these drawings and the last of them, *Boy with a pigeon*, is the masterpiece of Freud's adolescence. The pigeon sits quiet (but beadily quizzical, watchful) in the boy's hands. The extending lines of finger, wrist and sleeve cradle it, rocking a little; with the folds of suiting and shirting, they give the sheet a structure which possesses some of the repose that they enforce. The lumpiness of an unEnglish taste in outfitting and the tailored breadth support it. The mock-solemnity in a thick-necked carriage of the head is both the culmination of the shape, complacent in its presuming dominance, and also meditative, dreamy, poetic.

These early drawings are not always so masterlike but the confidence is essentially the same. The controlled, structured line led Freud at least once to a deliberately stylish picture

15

that was another step towards making painting an anthology of things that he liked, *Still life*

25 *with Chelsea buns*. The commonest of buns (but buns that have in his rendering an odd likeness to the shapes of waterlilies) were accompanied by a classical marble, a Janus head of quality. Drawing it, he outlined in areas the formalized modelling of the god. I had wondered sometimes how Freud came to fall so easily into an almost cloisonniste jigsaw in drawing the marble head. Then quite lately he showed me a whole portfolio of landscape watercolours of extraordinary quality which his father, who had done a year of art in Munich as part of his training, made among the Alpine lakes, apparently all in the year 1913. The facets of jewel-like colour in the tiny, brilliant, drawings were triangular, splinter-shaped, but the sophistication was essentially related. Not only the drawing of the still life, but the

8 background of *Landscape with birds*, and perhaps a constitutional precision in the joinery of Lucian's own style, all became a little easier to understand.

The confidently classical line, with the slightly narcissistic fondness for tailoring, reappeared in another of the free-association fantasies on his own likeness, *Man in a leather*

21 *coat*. The style itself was now quite self-regarding. The neat strips of hatching, parallel and criss-cross, along the lines were the beginning of Freud's preoccupation with systematic areas of pen-mark that build up sparkling codes for light. The neatly finished bands of hatching make *Man in a leather coat* quite a period piece, recalling the manner in which distinguished French painters of the more elegant kind imitated popular woodcuts. The stylized device was set, as only Freud would have set it (and did so again often in the years to come) against the irregular radiations of the iris, star-shaped and explosive, like an irresponsible little firework.

The most stylish of the paintings that collected things he liked, *Still life with Chelsea buns*, led to another picture of the same room in Abercorn Place and the same zinc-covered table.

33 With *Quince on a blue table*, the element of the bizarre in the whole idea of a collection of disparate treasures came to the top. One is almost ready to conclude that the choice was whimsical when the delicacy of the rendering persuades one of the real tenderness of his regard. In particular the delicacy with which he painted a favourite possession, a stuffed zebra's head which he had lately found the money to buy. The fruits, a paper bag or two crumpled into square-brushed, lucent facets, a stick of celery and a sugar-lump are capriciously assembled, but the painterly appreciation is consistent.

When Freud moved to a room of his own in Delamere Terrace, in the part of London, more or less, where he remained based for more than thirty years, the excitement prompted a

26 bigger and grander collection of the same kind, the biggest picture that he had painted. The selection was as miscellaneous as ever and the zebra's head, which was in fact cut short in the middle of the neck, with a ring that hung on a nail, now made its entry through a window contrived for the purpose. Freud explained recently, 'I wanted things to look possible, rather than irrational, if anything eliminating the surrealist look.' If that was really the purpose, the expedient was far from achieving it. The discrepancies between the items anthologized, in scale and style of rendering, gave the impression of an essay in the poetic surrealist vein. With

9, 23 the painter of *Village boys* and *Hospital ward*, the deduction was not necessarily justified. Received ideas of unity and consistency were already disposed of, however irrationally, by the

direct responses to feeling and taste. The surrealist appearance of the *Painter's room* was 26 confirmed by the elegance of the sofa – in fact brought from a junk shop round the corner – and the sense, indispensable to surrealism, of luxurious resources. The London Gallery was the first dealer with whom Freud had a contract. But he was very clear, he remembers, that he was not a surrealist. He thought that artistic groupings were ridiculous. 'Much as I admired early Chirico and Mirò, I objected to the fact that under the laws of doctrinaire surrealism as approved by Mesens it was easy for people of no talent to practise art.'

It is so long since Freud was thought of as in any superficial way a stylist that one forgets that growing up he was as proud as a peacock of his style in drawing and painting alike. It was a stylish time in British painting; Freud's contemporaries, liberated on the Mediterranean scene after years of insular austerity, admired and sought after as British painters had not been in living memory, were preening themselves and their modern-seeming styles. Freud on the whole did not admire them, but his painting temporarily reflected something deliberately stylish that was in the air – a sharpness of terminations, for example, a spiky, bristly consistency that conveyed intolerance of Romantic British picturesqueness. No one painted the disorder of ruffled plumage within such an impeccable edge, cut like a stencil. *Dead heron* takes on a quite heraldic simplicity and splendour. Silver light resolves the plumage into iridescent facets, modelling the shape as if the coherence of life was being reinvented. Tattered ends of feather and rumpled barbs fray into claw-like splinters, still quite clearly descended from the twigs and claws in *Landscape with birds*, but now with tragic overtones. The resolution is definite and unarguable without a sign of anything softened or spared.

Did Freud invent the mannered formulation of spiky vegetation that was de rigueur among the painters who went to Greece a year or two after he had drawn *Scotch thistle* in 1944? Very likely; I remember in the first of Freud's drawings that I saw in Charlotte Street years before, a quality that was a juvenile anticipation of *Rabbit on a chair* in the common style of 1944. The question is not even academic; the triumphs of precocity in the mid-forties have vanished away, too often in tragedies that do not bear recalling. Only Freud remains, with an achievement in which priority, at one point or another, is certainly the least interesting thing about it.

Once Freud borrowed a subject from a source which had left him remarkably unaffected in his formative years. Going to stay with Cedric Morris in 1943, he drew a group with *Cacti and stuffed bird* which Morris had set up to paint himself. The decorative taste is not quite like anything in Freud's own work. In his studio lately I have heard him remark, apropos of nothing, 'Do you know there is something called picture-making? I think it is often simply fatigue. It rules out the hope of making something remarkable.'

By comparison with the fashionable picture-making of the time, Freud's work of the later forties was full of energy, necessity and an ambition, precisely, to make something remarkable. Black pen marks stab the white paper into luminous colour. Light had a part to play in what was to come, precision and sharpness even more so. In Greece in 1946 Freud painted miniature still-lifes of a *Lemon sprig* and an *Unripe tangerine*, again with its twig and leaves. They were outlined against the light with a sharpness that was hallucinatory. Something spectral remained from the poetics of the zebra pictures but now it was observed in actuality. A picture had become, and perhaps in a sense still is, a unique order of apparition, a spectre of the real. One remembers the little pictures as sharpened by their minuteness, as if to pierce the eye and haunt it. Sharpened equally by the penetrating authenticity, which made them irresistible and captivating.

We are made aware in these pictures, as we do not reckon to be if we have thought of art as an invitation to the nebulous, of distinctness as a quality in itself. The abruptness, the sudden changes of direction in living shape, are themselves favourite qualities to be collected and treasured. They are keys to credibility, self-verifying qualities of the actual. In 1947, when the

(continued following plate II)

pictures were seen at the London Gallery, one could already suspect that these edgy tokens of what really exists were taking us into country unlike any other in modern art, where the everyday purposes and incentives are not prevented or abashed but still pay off in the rewarding currencies we live by. In fact, they were in general found perplexing. 'What are we to say about Lucian Freud?' Herbert Read asked himself a few years later, when they reappeared with the pictures that followed them at the Venice Biennale ' – Lucian Freud, the Ingres of Existentialism.' It remains nevertheless about the best comment on Freud to this day.

We might have noticed that in Freud's work of these years not only were people becoming more prominent, retaining in art more of the attention that they get naturally outside it, in the house or the street, but they were reappearing. One woman appeared three or four times, first when Freud was twenty in a drawing in which the mood of preoccupation, anxiety perhaps, haunting a face, similarly and sympathetically occupied the image. Two years later there were *29* little paintings of her, cut like sculptured busts by a table edge, each with a flower, a daffodil or a tulip, under her gaze, with eyes wide-open, devouring, or else turned inward, half-closed, brooding. She was no one I recognized, as I said lately, not admitting to curiosity, leaving the *32, 34* question unasked. Freud answered quietly, preoccupied himself perhaps, 'She was the first person who meant something to me.' As if overhearing, I was not sure that I should hear. The tone of voice, rather than the words, made me realize that we were talking about the beginning of a kind of painting, as well as of a kind of meaning. Another day, Freud explained, 'I wanted to convey that she was the first person I was really caught up with.' We were talking both about a kind of involvement, which was inseparable from painting, painting that made questions and answers about *who* inviting, yet useless and inadmissable, excluded by the new and total reference of painting from life. I should not have expected words to add anything to the intensity, which is beyond verbalization. An actuality by turns splendid, voracious and withdrawn, is entitled to precedence over identification or explanation or words – over everything, that is to say, but the sparing paint of these minimal, irreducible portrayals, which alone contribute to our knowledge of the meanings that people may hold for us, that of which (as the philosopher wrote, whom Freud has often in mind) we cannot speak.

(continued following plate 37)

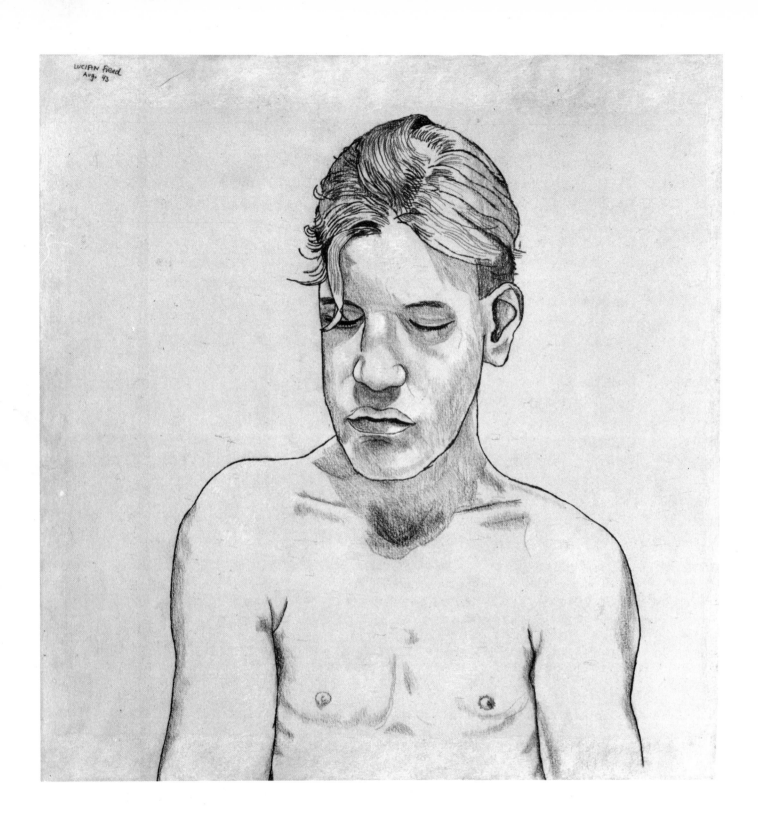

20 i 43

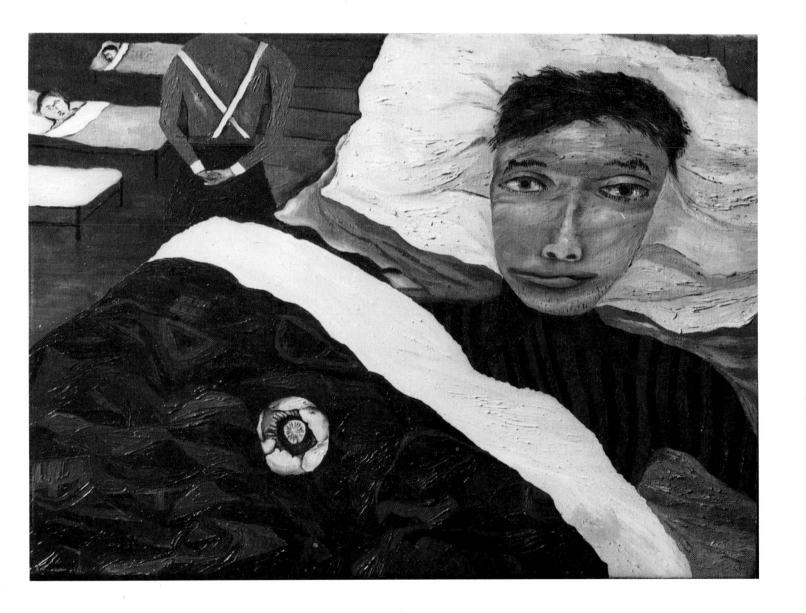

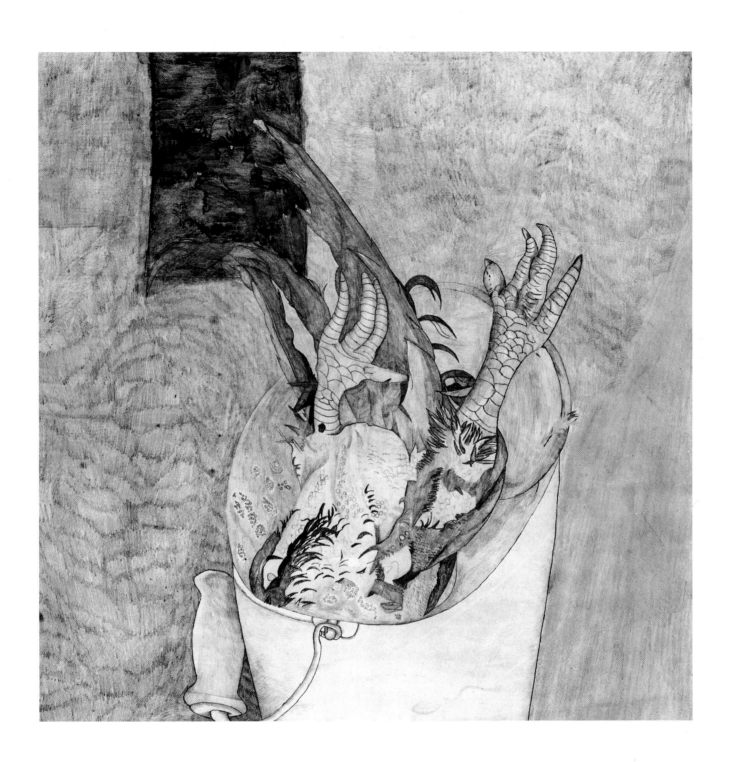

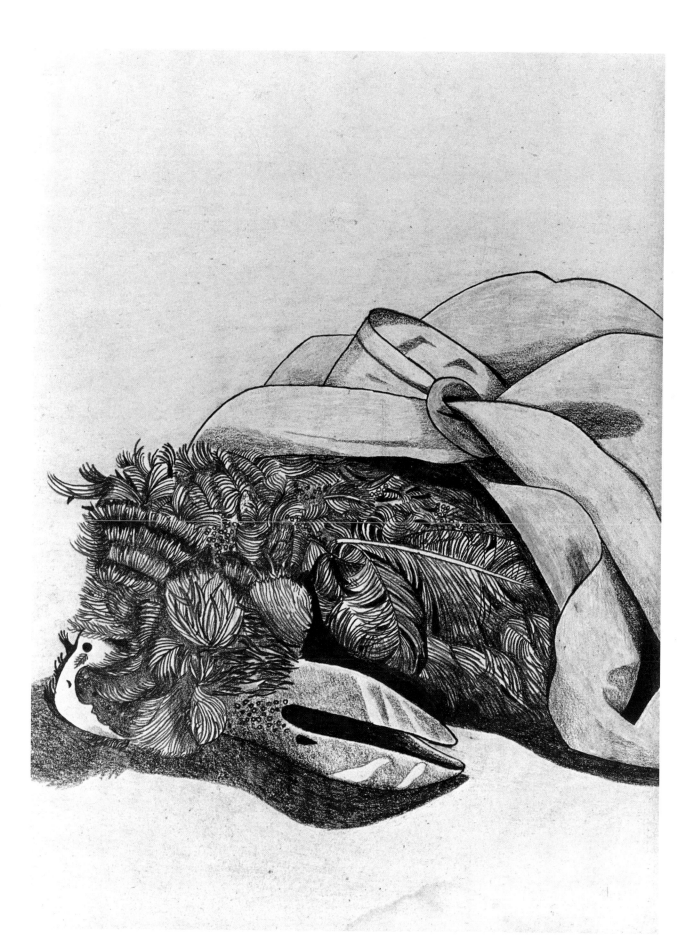

April 44

Lucian Freud

From this point on, Freud's painting is essentially about people. There are townscapes with a sense of habitation and the litter inseparable from urban life; there are equally urban interiors, with the plants that flourish in them. Otherwise the subjects are all people, people who submitted to be painted. They are people who have a regard for the painter; it is apparent in their faces. He apparently knows them well; it is a matter of principle with him to paint like a native, not a tourist. 'If you don't know them,' he remarked lately, 'it can only be like a travel book'. The majority of them have been part of his life. A very few may have come to him for a portrait in the usual way; he seems always to have become involved with them and engaged with the human look of them. This concern penetrated immediately into the pictures. Later it has more and more suffused the paint and communicated itself through it. The fact that Freud has never been unconcerned with any of the people he paints is enough to make him, believe it or not, almost unique among painters. Only a few of the greatest have invariably been involved as he is. From the moment at twenty-four when he came to this kind of painting, he brought to it a man's impulses and reactions, not greatly censored, flattered or disguised, but more or less intact, a human disposition very much as it came, left to mark the paintings as it would.

In this situation, a writer has no recourse but to tell simply what he knows and does not know about the achievement. It is exceptional not only in its positive qualities but in what is absent. There is no padding, no commentary, there are no signs of what is customary in studios and none of the conventional preconceptions which load the record one way or another in nearly all of what painting from life exists.

The picture is bare, just the paint and canvas; we are told nothing about it. The titles are unindicative; they no more than confirm what we can see. Though these transactions with people and paint have obviously been a man's life, there is no biography or autobiography attached. Few of his models are identified. Chiefly painters, whom we know anyway, and a photographer who worked with them. Otherwise only his mother, who has been painted ten times, some (not all) of his children, who are named 'because I thought they might like it', and a friend in Soho to encourage him. Apart from these, no one. Yet the identities are not unimportant. (Perhaps they are too important.)

If we were curious about these people, we could learn or guess something from the number of times that Freud has painted them. It would appear that his relationship with some of them has been close. We may deduce this or imagine it – we shall never know it, except by chance. If we were told, the only effect would be to displace the real theme. The effect of compiling a cast list for the play that is a painter's world and subject – one can test it with the lists of names that are attempted for pictures like Courbet's *Atelier* – is to blind one to the inherent life of painting. If we were told about the wide array of the people more or less 'in his life' that Freud has been painting for thirty-five years – I like to think of it as an allégorie réelle – the effect would be to alter *us*, the way gossip columns do: curiosity is one of the appetites that grow with feeding. If we were told, it would only distract and detract from the knowledge that we can and do get from painting and nowhere else, from no other source whatsoever.

(continued following plate 40)

20 I 44

This kind of painting represents what can be seen of a human being, and also the character of the seeing. Sight is not just one of the senses. It is *the* sense, the faculty with which a person construes his environment and other people. So the character of his seeing is the character of a person's way with the world, the most personal property there is. By the mid-1940s Freud was painting people who meant something to him – at the same time he showed the quality of a very close and personal scrutiny, which was intimately his and intimate with them, yet in its truthfulness detached. The pictures are representations both of seeing and of being seen, on the part of the model and painter alike. The woman who was painted with a tulip and her successors devoured with their eyes, sometimes with a steady ferocity. Yet with the same wide-open look they made themselves vulnerable, as children do in their game of staring, trying to make one another look away in self-protection. They were laying themselves open, while the painter devoured them: the willingness they disclose in themselves is as plain as their own voracity; it must be one of the subjects of their own simultaneous, smouldering, inward look. Visually devouring him, we may guess that they are also indulging, and fearing, the dream of being devoured. He is certainly realizing a fantasy of visual possession and he is re-enacting a sense of the direction and coherence of each form. He is (one can watch it when he is working) following an intuition of what the forms of life require, what attention, what faithfulness in recreating the principle that moulds bodily shape from inside. In 1950 this was chiefly in the future. With Freud's paintings of the sixties and seventies I am reminded that he told me, 'If you look at the forms, it is clear that some of them want to be liberated.'

When Freud was drawing me for an etching, I realized how deeply for him representation was still affected by the habit of gathering the things he liked. I was puzzled that he did not draw verifiably from a fixed position, which he could depend on returning to. He answered that for him it was more like aiming than copying. Very sharp sight is not needed to point at the model the signal that will bounce and register; I had the impression of a process rather like echo-sounding. The shapes feel their way, and find their places by making room for one another. 'I take readings', Freud said, 'from a number of positions because I don't want to miss anything that could be of use to me. I often put in what is round the corner from where I see it, in case it is of use to me. It soon disappears if it is not. Towards the end I am trying to get rid of absolutely everything I can do without. Ears have disappeared before now.'

Imaginative people become unused to responding to anything that is not imaginary. Talking about a figurative painter who is not only living but alive, as only one or two painters are at any time, I feel a desperate duty to shake the critical language till it gasps, massage and kiss the prostrate faculties until with a shudder they draw a groaning breath, and tell how precious is the awareness that this one kind of painting, straight from the living subject, can supply. And extraordinary – in no other tradition, no other culture, with no lesser moral imperative, only with this commitment to the lively truth of painting is it even imaginable.

It has to be imagined, this image of what is humanly seen in a human subject. It is not copied, but re-imagined from life. People talk and painters paint as if figurative painting possessed only a contingent magic, holding meaning by nature's permission – as if the significance resided in the dependence, the ratio to an indubitable naturalness, like a

(continued following plate 61)

47, 48

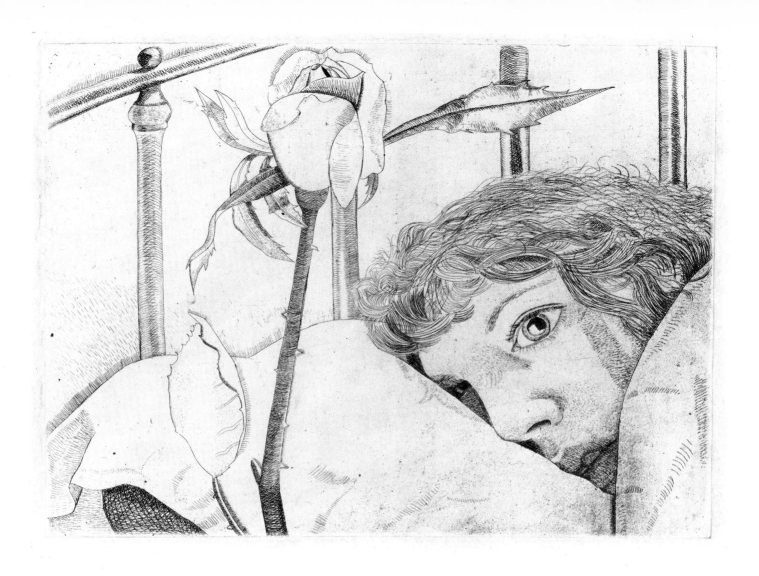

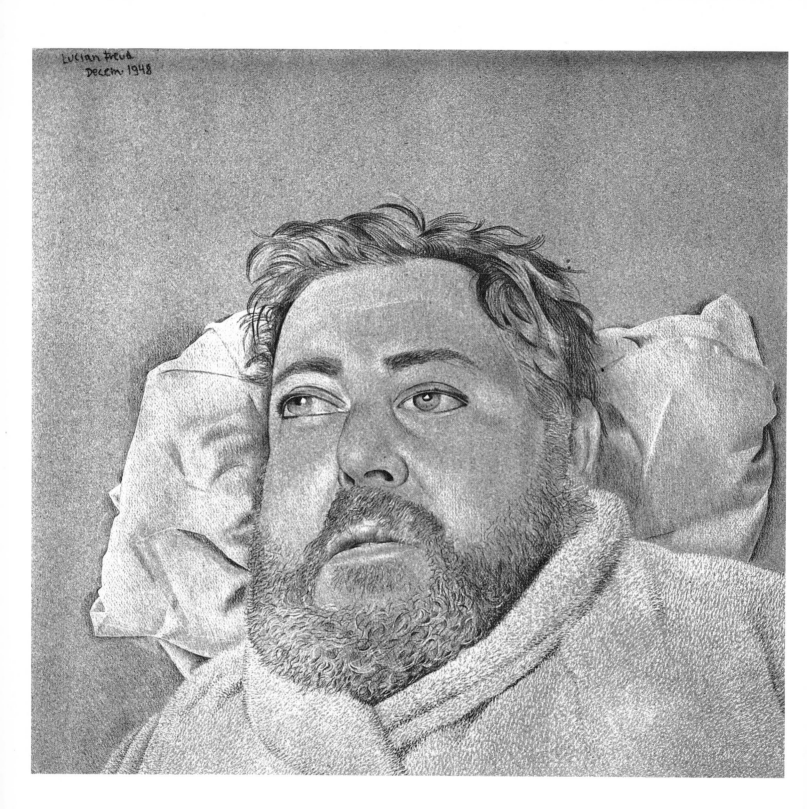

55, 56

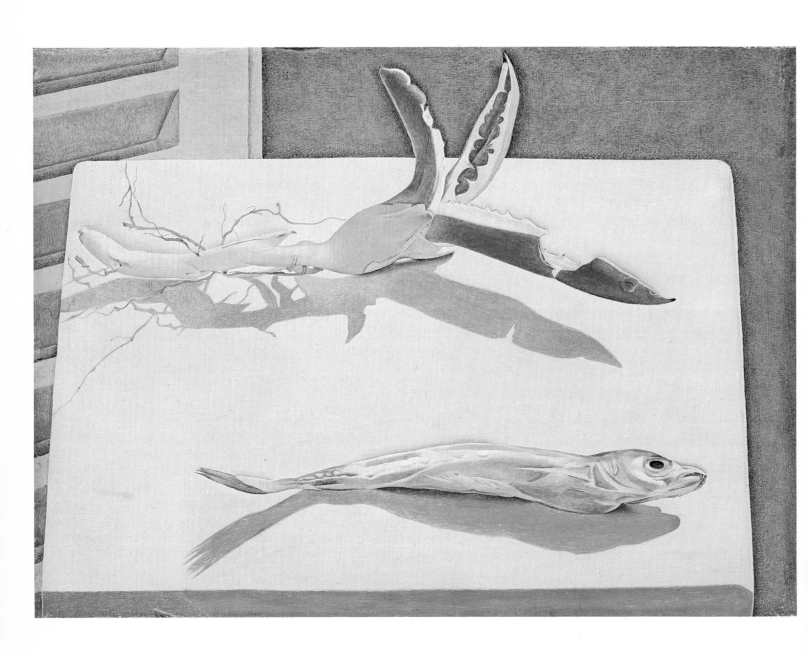

perpetual impressionistic obedience, without authority of its own. It was the view that demeaned the autonomy of art – and damaged the prospects for representation and visual faithfulness in the twentieth century. Lucian Freud has from the beginning been entirely aware of the spell that is the property of the image in itself, the property that returns it to the timeless independence of imaginative art.

The paintings of the dark girl, naturally unnamed but never unrecognized, with wide eyes in her heart-shaped face and hair spreading into curly tendrils, were the centre of Freud's achievement in his twenties. For a few years from 1947 she dominated his work, and was eventually drawn nursing their baby on a page that was for once idyllic and enraptured. The five or six pictures built up an image as unforgettable as a myth. It must have been their finish and poise, which have a kind of perfection, that prompted Read's fancy of an Ingres for Existentialism, and Ingres, the patron saint of modern classicism, has always been among the masters whom Freud valued highest. A critic, who has never been forgiven for mistaking his idol for David, teased him viciously by finding something primitive in his literalness. The presence of Ingres in Freud's pantheon was enough to show that so far from being ingenuous, he took his classicism at full strength; like Ingres, who spoke of probity, Freud was set on the intellectual and moral dignity of art. The information that he assembled was certainly literal; indeed it had an actuality in itself. The deposit of detail, flat on the surface, used to remind one of deposits spread on the shore by the tide. That was its grace; it had the consistency, the homogenous, even legibility and a sea-washed cleanliness which are qualities of the naturalistic deposit at its purest. They did not come about by chance; Freud was very conscious, he has told me, of the consistent distribution of information, and the difficulty of securing it. The internal economy of representation has been his study all his life.

These pictures were seen almost at once to be a sustained and concentrated feat that no one had supposed to be within the reach of a British painter in his twenties, least of all one whom opinion classified as 'serious' and 'modern'; the critical distinctions of 1950 now seem antique. Qualities of the figurative skills may have distinguished good painters a hundred years earlier, but never since; so the conventional wisdom went. It was if anything incidental, incidental to the achievements of Picasso himself, secondary in the appeal of Giacometti. The French painters who had turned to figuration with the encouragement of Derain had a certain dank poetry, but were their qualities specifically figurative? There was doubt whether the evident quality of Freud could rest on anything so humdrum as the quality of the representation; it would have been just that which puzzled Herbert Read. Everything that Freud has painted since 1950 has, incidentally, been by way of answering exactly this question, and it must be said that criticism, what there is of it, has been far from alert in taking up his testimony.

Categories and reputations are not the serious matter of art. If we are to say what it was that seriously distinguished these pictures, it cannot have been only the new-found skills or the finish that contrived to look neatly modern. It was rather a quality of confidence, a trust. The painter showed he could rely on the figurative reflex and its superfine conditioning, rely in fact on the serenity of his command to accommodate not only the visible subject but the

50
48, 49, 52,
56, 59

inward tension, the subject that was not serene at all, the emotional juncture that stretched to the limit the proportionate composure of a face and left the extremity nakedly displayed. There was no violence, no expressionism, nothing German; no memory of Die neue Sachlichkeit rose to vex the lucid reading. This objectivity was the timeless kind, which has always been able to include the outward shape and the internal situation together and entire. The symmetry was disturbed only a little; the dislocation was quite slight. No doubt it was involuntary, inherent in the totality of the observation and the conviction of the report. The mood, the content, was held in suspense; it is as if the model held her breath. It seems impossible that she should not have been trembling. A painter, or rather, *this* painter – I do not know where to find his like since the great ages of trust in the multiple truthfulness of art – recreates a person in terms of otherwise inaccessible knowledge. In the cold light of the Ingriste formulation, the flatness with rondures, it is seen that beauty (and this model is presented as one of the most beautiful in painting) consists in the state of being bare of defences. Love is the condition of being at one another's mercy. The girl's capacity for suffering must serve for both; we guess this couple works it overtime. The remorseless sharpness of the focus on her eyes reveals them, each time in a new dimension, minutely displaced. They are perpetually watchful for an emergency that is inevitable. The hunger and pain in them are mixed always with apprehension, which is worse. No one could miss it, yet no one else could wholly understand.

There was something dandified about the impeccable persona reflected in these pictures. More so, it may be, than agrees with self knowledge. In the drawing called *Man at night*, the 55 self-image has a dazzling sparkle, which is not only a matter of the perfection of the systematic pen-mark codes for tone, which stipple the shadow, knit the collar, round the cheek with its reflections and weave the velvet darkness behind him. It is all very perfect, but the style as well as the face wears a mean look. One cannot require an artist to be generous with himself. But one may feel that Freud tells more that is to his purpose and ours on the frequent occasions when he loses himself altogether in someone else. Such was the occasion on which he drew one of the best portrait drawings of the century, the head of *Christian Bérard*, ailing and 53 querulous yet immense in his authority, a Czar of style (such as Freud could understand). Did anyone ever see Bérard more entirely himself? A sense of the entirety of a person, and the principle that moulds him, is Freud's longest-lasting, most original theme. It evokes a graphic faculty near to illustration, yet insistently deeper than that, a quality that one meets with recognition, for example, when the curling, sparing touch persuades the paper to live and to radiate the life of its subject. Is it the light and atmosphere round a castle among trees, evoked from paper by gentle, wide-spaced pen strokes in a drawing by Bruegel that rises to mind? I am startled that the comparison occurs to me, because I count Bruegel beyond compare. Another work, as it happens, that I have felt through the decades since I saw it, soon after it was etched, to be in a sense quite separate from its illustrative vividness, incomparable in British art, is called *Ill in Paris*. It is the title for an illustration; even someone without liking 51 for the genre may be moved if a lover has been unwell in a French hotel. When his partner took to her bed, prostrate and trembling, with beside her a thorny rose, like a fairy-tale emblem of the relationship, Freud's reaction was to go out for a grounded etching plate and nitric acid. The pharmacist tried to dissuade him from a crime of passion. One can sympathize with the forebodings both of the chemist and of the invalid. The plate was etched in the washbasin, fumes curling upwards. The meeting in this print of a classic economy and a sentiment that is held in suspense link it only with the graphic poetry in the first, moving etchings of the century.

Faced with an oeuvre, so largely unlabelled and unnamed, which evidently has unfolded what was most enticingly private in a life, the reader may be forgiven for wondering when the writer will get round to specifying who was what and when. Is it possible that this acquaintance of the artist really *does not know*? A few years ago, at Freud's exhibition, I was in front of that moving, ultimate image – as I read it – of what is essentially perilous and necessarily heart-breaking in love, called *Last portrait*. (What knowledge of who was actually 142 who could add in the slightest to a title like that?) The curiosity bursting out, to be recognized in the same instant as useless, doing no service to what I value in painting or myself, I asked a friend, who had known both the painter and me, for a clue to the story. The friend is sensibly suspicious of me; when we were colleagues she picked her way gingerly through my ramparts of verbosity. She turned incredulously. 'Do you really not know?' I did not and do not. I know instead that if I had managed to gratify my curiosity, then I should have cheated myself of the essence of that picture, that quite specific, definite, unmysterious thing, which lacks nothing, that lovely masterpiece of love. Suppose I sentimentally misread the picture. Does it matter so long as there is such a picture? The picture is unaffected; it can never lose its value or withdraw what it contributed to a realization that is humanly entire and entirely human. With the inevitability of human ambivalence on its head, it will testify forever to the simultaneous rock-steadiness and inconstant quicksilver mobility of a man. We have only to read from it the integrity of the figurative impulse to feel quite incurious about the unheard anecdote, to be quite content that the story was no other than whatever it was.

What I know about all this – whether knowledge or lack of it – is significant only as untouched evidence of what an acquaintance of the painter happened to hear or not hear about a life that can have been hardly separable from some of the best, because most intimate, painting of its time. Did I not know any of these sitters who evidently played a part in Freud's life? Yes, one. Imagine me, if you want the story, out to dinner years later, and there, in the context of another marriage and another art, I meet the woman with the heart-shaped face and spreading tendrils. We talk; I am aware, as if of a picture, of the wide-eyed look, and find her in fact charmingly prepared, not for flight, but for the small-talk of artistic life. She is interested to hear that I have written about her first husband. I promise to send the piece to her, and realize, from the way on parting she reminds me, that this memory and these pictures remain in the forefront of her mind, as they do in the painter's – the painter who denies that he ever looks back, yet is at once alert when he hears that someone has met her. The truth is that any other impression of this beautiful woman and every other experience of hers are no more than appendages to the central thing, which is the fact of these five or six pictures – an unshakeable fact that we all retain, secure in the image stock that remains from the time we have lived through. The girl with the heart-shaped face is interested; the no longer so casual acquaintance promises to send. He intends to find the cutting, means to post it and fails to do a thing about it. To break the promise is a betrayal and he feels guilty about Kitty from that day to this.

The name is no one's business, nothing to do with the pictures. It slips out, yet the slip need not mark the tablet on which the knowledge specific to painting should register. A mimimal identification percolates to a minority of the audience in this small world of art. The lack of any label would hinder in identifying, not the sitter – she has vanished back into the mythology of great pictures – but in identifying an element in Freud's art that was owed to her image and remained to affect others, till this image almost hindered the faithfulness that he brought the next. If faithfulness is the word. What other word is there for the fidelity that is the virtue of portrayal, a virtue that is as lasting as painting? Painting and its models are very lasting. They are for the ages, perpetual and unbetrayed.

(continued following plate 69)

64

By 1950 Freud was making the human image alive and precise as modern painting had never been. The adjectives are his; the aim (not the claim) was quite explicit. Painting a portrait a little later, he found the mouth and nose in his picture *alive and precise* in a way that the rest was not; he became conscious that he was trying to stop a look of Kitty in the eyes. Vision and style were due for radical changes, but they do not seem to have been related, as with some painters, to a change of companionship or model. The last of the pictures of Kitty, *Girl with a white dog* in the Tate, was roundly modelled in the new manner. Earlier, Kitty had *59* always been painted in full light. It was needed for the flattening of form in the Ingriste formulation, and for the modulation that rounded form along the contour. Now the subject was to be modelled in light and shadow. Characteristically, half the form was darkened, or lighted only by the play of reflections. The subtle and continuous tempering in variations of colour and value was wrought with an observant delicacy, with nothing schematic or summary or defiant. The mood was rather attentive and responsive: the means, at the opposite extreme from the cool opacity of the Kitty pictures, was a refined and persuasive stippling of warm, thin colours with a sable brush.

Before the painter had usually been engrossed in the image of a single person who filled the picture; in the early fifties there is more than once a theme, if only the elaborate evocation of a milieu, which is more or less deliberately enigmatic. In one there is a man in a raincoat in a room with a palm. It owes a curious emptiness to the size, twice as big as anything that Freud *66* painted before or for another seventeen years; nevertheless, it remains a portrait, in the transverse light that now suited him, with no more or less illustrative content, apart from the look of a particular sitter, than *Girl with a white dog* painted immediately after it. At the time it had the quality of a defiant manifesto of his belief in the universal applicability of his enigmatically objective terms of reference.

If Freud was being forced to the difficult discovery that his real subject was the visible shape of people, usually one at a time, uncluttered by illustration or omen, examined as closely as he liked, that subject offered all the meanings and mysteries of the world. His new model, a blonde with a round face and tilted nose seemed no more at ease than the last. *Girl in bed* opened her eyes as wide as Kitty's, but with a naked vulnerability that was if anything less defended, more painful. Being painted in itself is hardly endurable; *Girl in bed* has bitten *72* her finger nails. *Girl in a green dress* seems at odds with the painter in some indefinite, *74* unassuageable way. Yet the ordeal is fruitful. The detail is finer, more silken than ever; it almost weaves the spell that model and painter are awaiting. The development is one of increasing desperation. In *Hotel bedroom* the model has in turn taken to her bed, nervous *78* fingers held to her cheek, while the painter waits darkly beyond. Yet their problem does not seem open to any violent resolution. Perhaps they are simply re-enacting the unforgettable scene of *Ill in Paris*. Sure enough, some of its ominous magic descends on them once again. *51* Very likely the painter and the intimates whom he was painting were tormented only by the discovery that the profound and lasting meanings of figure painting are not within reach of dramatic illustration. So at any rate, it has turned out for Freud. His image of the rather few people whom he knows very well indeed becomes the theatre for his realization of what it entails for us to be both physically and imaginatively present to each other.

(continued following plate 87)

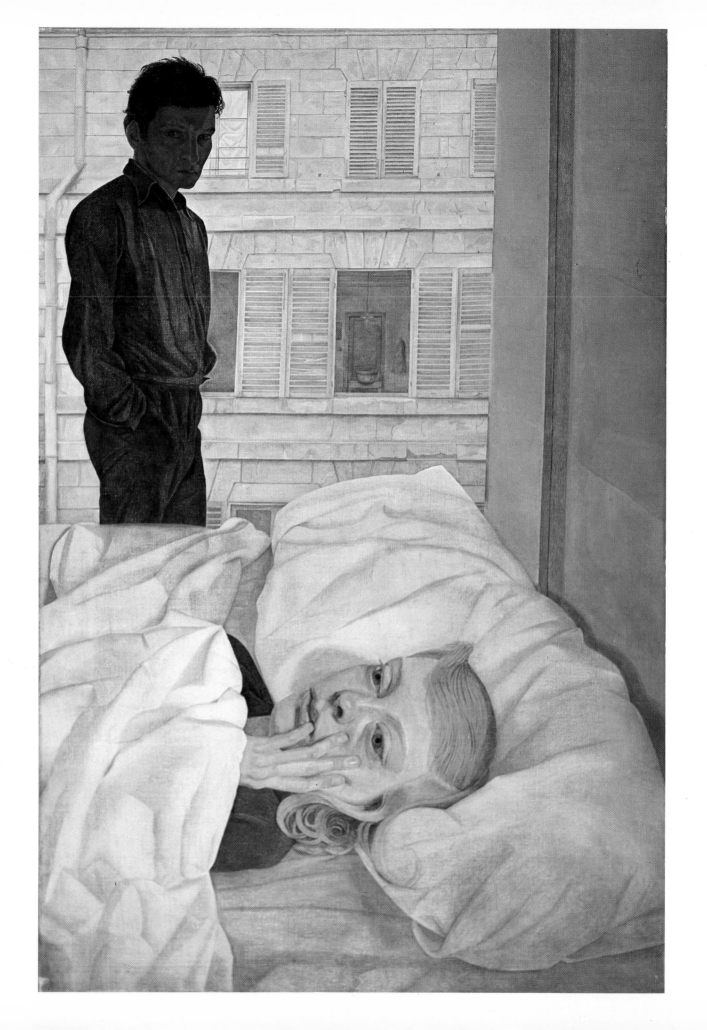

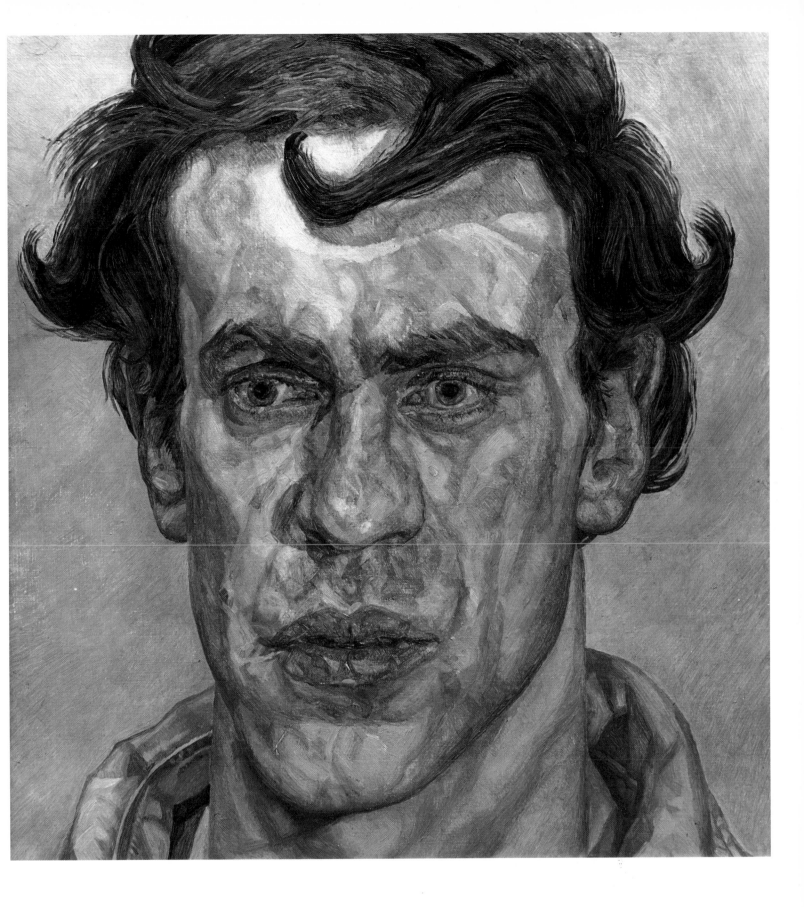

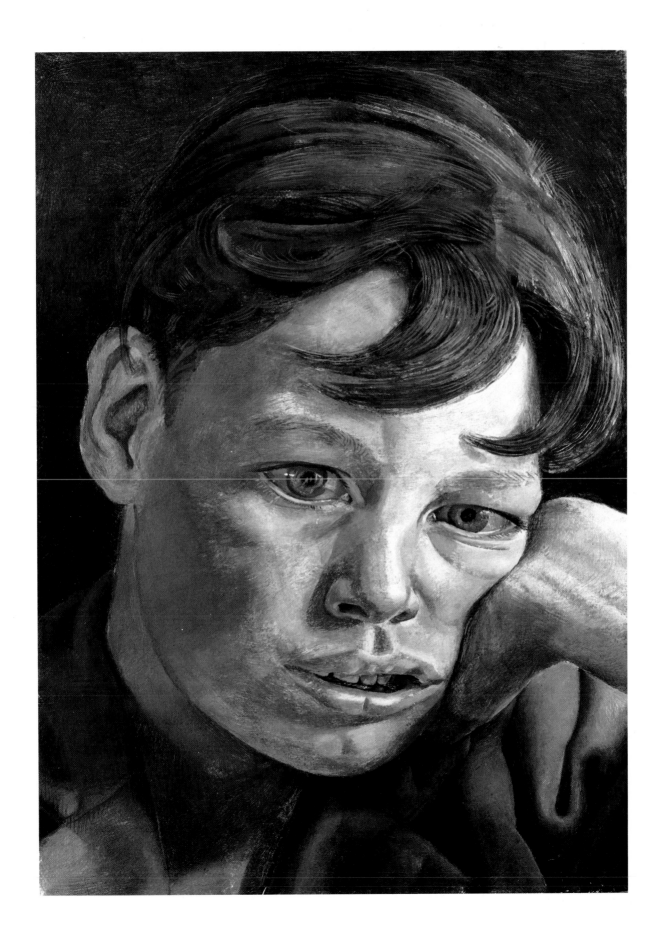

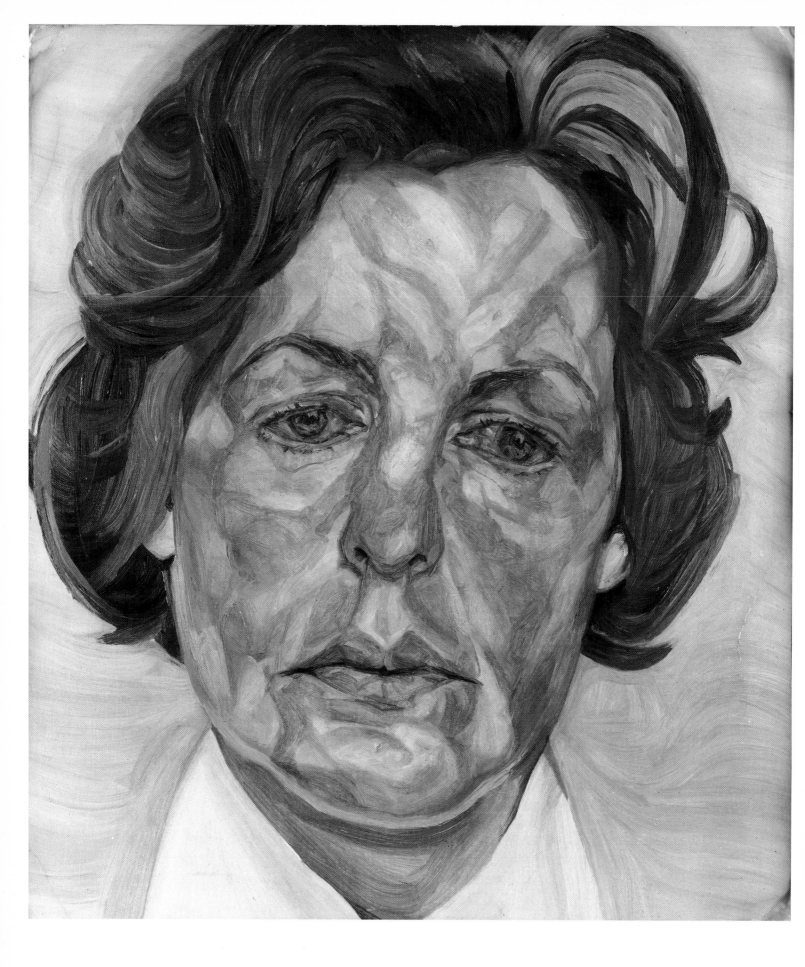

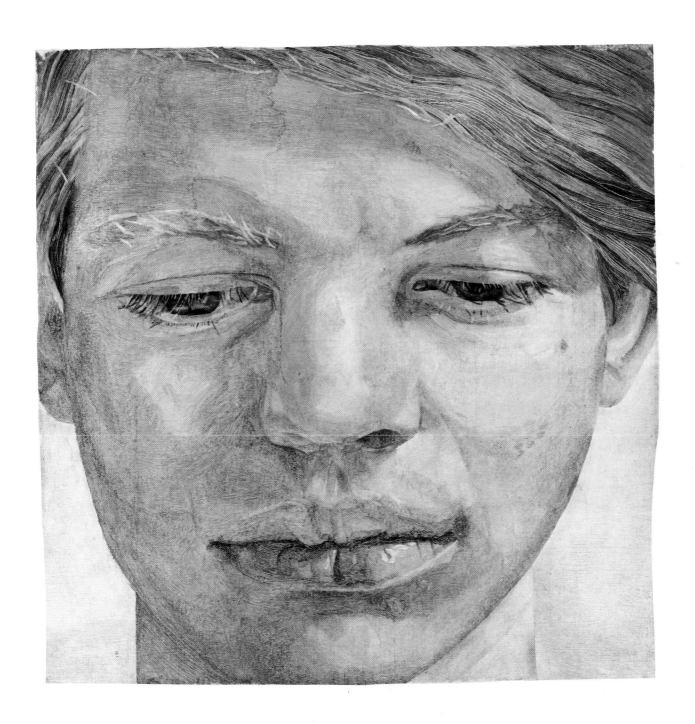

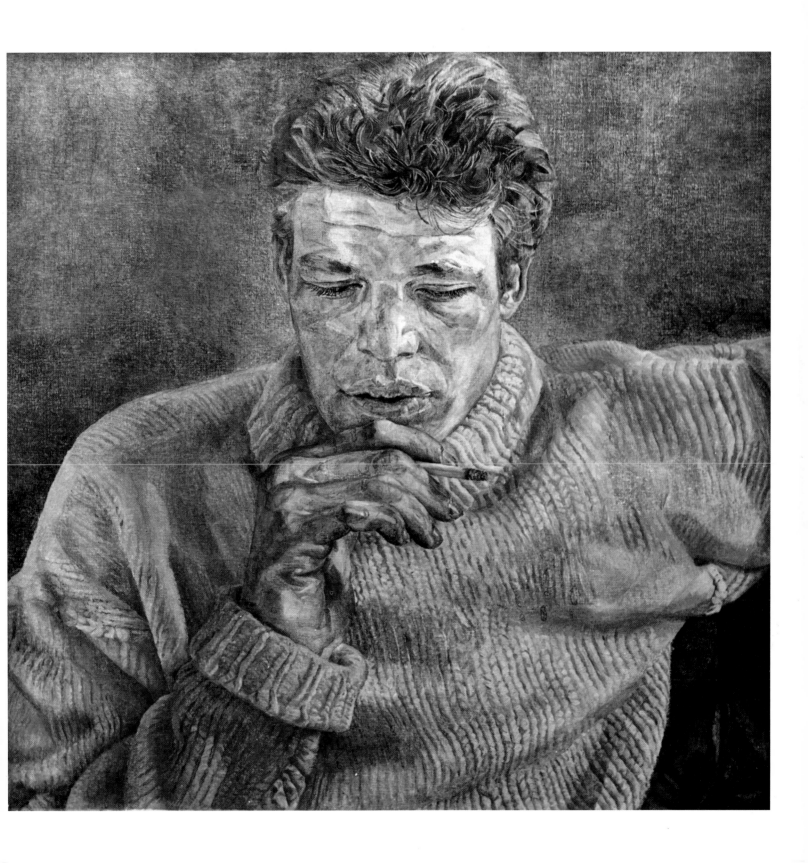

To judge by these naked, bloodshot eyes Freud was still high on the intimacies of vision. Perhaps simply on intimacy: in more than one of the pictures of the time it is the closeness
67   with which we know the most minute and private shapes that strike us. With *A woman painter*, for example, seeing under the eyelid to its delicate lining, raised a little away from the eyeball, one thinks only of how undefended the woman is, portrayed in a mood of resignation, which is one's first impression, before anything visual. The privacy of the eye is echoed by the colour under the lock of hair that overlaps the forehead. We find courage in her face. Freud must have been willing from early on that painting should be found embarrassing, and thought of this as a positive quality. Perhaps a modern quality, a reversal of the terms of tradition, which are now so far out of reach, yet so much desired by Freud, and better understood by him than ever in the recent past. In the detail of his most faithful, most real portrayal, he was capable in the mid fifties of being more seriously, more embarrassingly surreal than anyone since the first surrealists.

The probing intimacy was taking on a particular force because Freud's style had never been so confident in its spare economy, so graceful and athletic. The draughtsman was relaxed as the painter could not be. There is nothing better in modern drawing than the sleepy weight of
75   his blond sitter's head. This was the time that Freud painted what turned out to be the first of his portraits of a noble family, which when they were exhibited together with the great collection that the generations have assembled at Chatsworth, their house, gave a most convincing demonstration of how one of our contemporaries may measure against achievements of the masters, and the best reason for pride. The extrovert attentiveness to textures, the lustre and sparkle in the hair of brows and lashes and the jewel-like mottling of
71   pupils are nowhere better than in the earliest of the Chatsworth pictures. At least as satisfactory, when you see it in the context of the tradition at its finest, is this evidence that a capacity to take the opportunities of the portrait trade, without reducing in the slightest the serious depth of his own view, may be one of the talents that eventually make a very good painter better than good. Among the Chatsworth pictures one may find that one does not say very much to the purpose about Freud without saying something about Rembrandt too.

The ductile yet positive touch he brought to paint, on an unassuming scale very often, but with confidence and justice, equipped him for a marvellous group of little portraits painted with the finished quality of the past on etching plates. A miniature of himself that is smaller
62   still catches him in the most winning and earnest self-searching. In the enlargement here the picture itself well supports the same scrutiny. Best of all, and best known, the portrait of
64   Francis Bacon is the most even and judicious deposit of pictorial information in all his work. It is the rare essence of northern painting, this consistency in the mastery of the particular that the grandeur of ideal generality never beats.

Freud's achievement at thirty convinced everyone but himself. The Bacon portrait, hanging in the Tate, quite unobtrusive, yet biting like a little serpent when it caught you, exerted the transfixing spell of an image that is tantamount to the thing itself. The fact that a portrayal could work an original transformation, yet remain indisputable and objective in a new way, made and makes a deep impression, comparable in these respects with the sitter's own

(continued following plate 92)

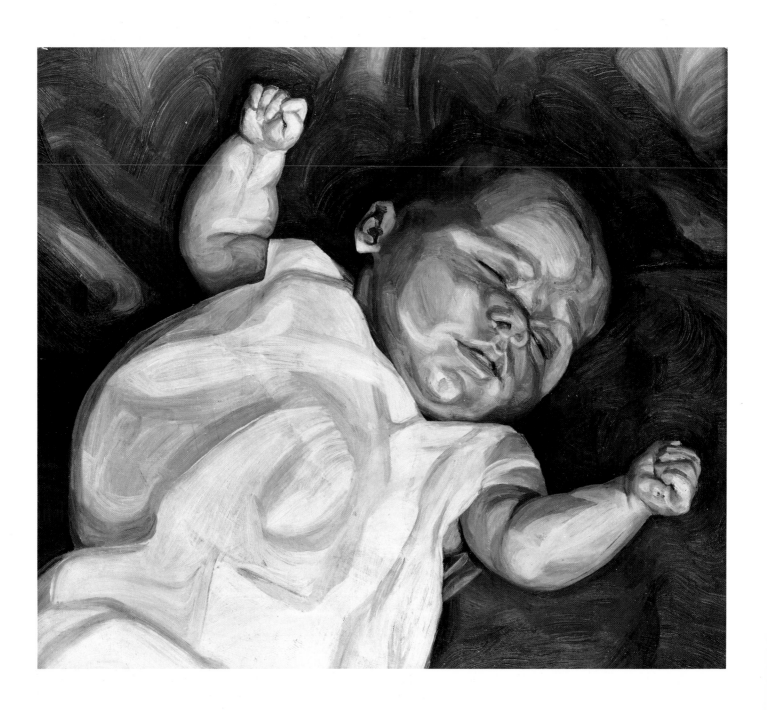

89, 90

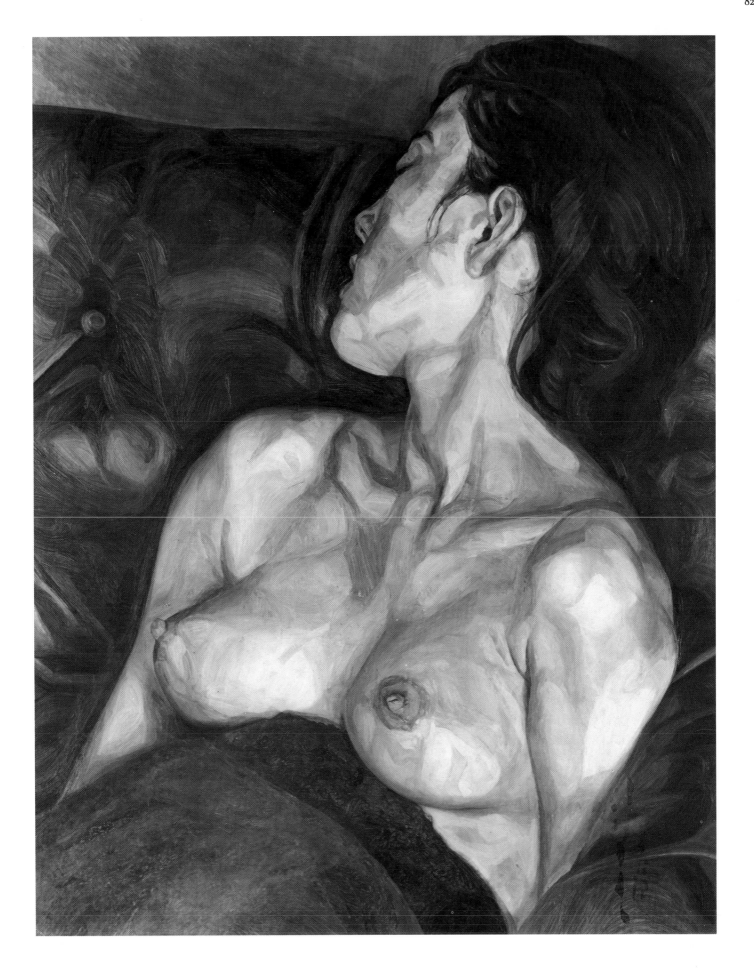

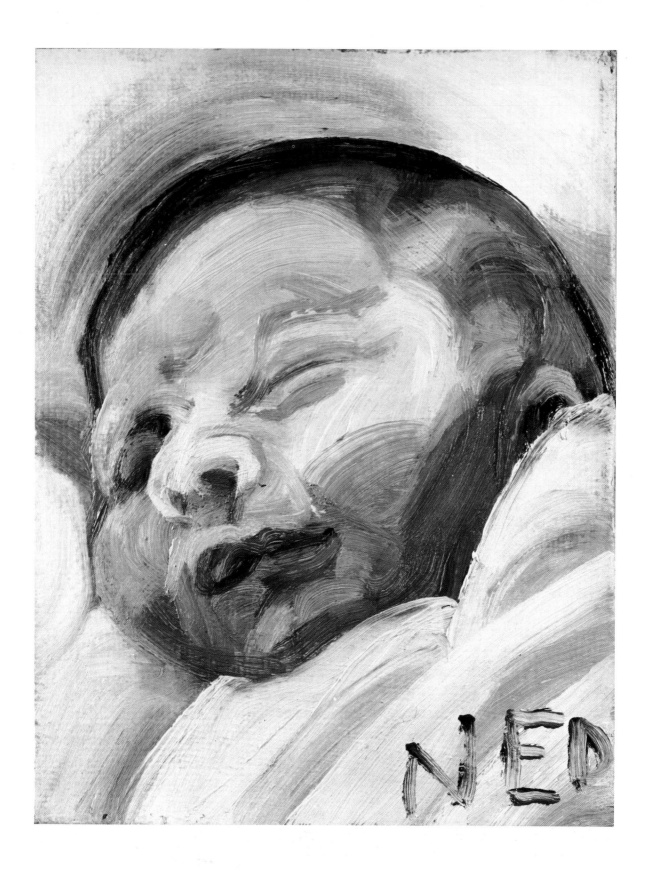

redefinition of painting. In these respects and no others; in every other way the little head is utterly different, turning the stomach just the other way, with an authenticity in the portrayal which was a rebuttal and infuriating for being so. Francis Bacon is a unique animal and unparalleled in his definition of painting perhaps by virtue of being so. It was wonderful that Freud could round the swelling cheek, so that the ear fell so flatly and characteristically back, and taper the sloping temple with just this character of uniqueness. But how? Not exclusively visually, it would seem, not optically, obviously not photographically, nor indeed graphically, nor measurably, nor sculpturally. Rather, I should guess, it was done through a quite physical apprehension of the bodily proximity of the sitter, a lunging, imaginative probing that located the whereabouts of strangeness, and by a sense that is no one else's, assessed a displacement of air and light other than its own.

Looking closely at the Bacon portrait one was then perhaps already aware – it may have been a part of its unaccountable eeriness – of a constructive power that was stirring in the distinctness of shapes, a power, for example, that was visibly recreating the nose out of discrete constituents. The unity – an integral sense of poise, a balance in the phenomena that constitute *head* – was still undisturbed. It was in the painting of a woman, where most things happen in Freud's work, that the break-through came. With *Woman smiling*, though the poise was still perfect, the constructive energy was liberated. Everything in the previous pictures had been quite specific. Now the variations of colour no longer necessarily stood for separable things. For the moment paint did not have to be so specific. The mottling of colour rather rendered elements that made up the form, and rendered them with an inherent energy. These wedges of colour were expressions of purpose in the paint and in the flesh, the paint that was driven across the surface with the springy bristles of a hog-hair brush quite unlike the touch of the pliant sable, which had followed the forms with obedient literalness.

68

Freud's work has been concerned with this kind of impulse ever since, with the fullness of form and the bodily life shining through it. For once, one can perhaps connect the change with a splendid sitter. She had never appeared before and she was not seen again for more than twenty years. There is a coherence in her pose which leaves us believing that for her the head shares in the body's life with a natural integration that is enjoyed. When she appears again, still looking down at herself in the same fulfilled mood, in the big picture that is on the easel as I write, the coherence is recognizable again.

Talking about these elements that come together to make up the living shape I have seen Freud bring the finger-tips of one hand together, like three or four segments of a cone, as he explained how a bunch of muscles like little buttresses press inward to build together a nose or a chin. Just similarly the wedges of colour or, as often in *Woman smiling*, thinning of colour, radiant with light from the ground, lean together to build living volume. They compose so distinctly, the segments of form and the cornerwise residues between them. The colour is so clear, and then so deep where it was left unlightened in the creases that anchor the roundness, dimple it, link it to skeletal symmetries and then loose it where its richness can flourish with her natural good humour. It is so distinct and so clear that the result is entirely finite, recognizable and undoubted. And yet in another sense it is mysterious; the sequences

(continued following plate 106)

102, 103, 104

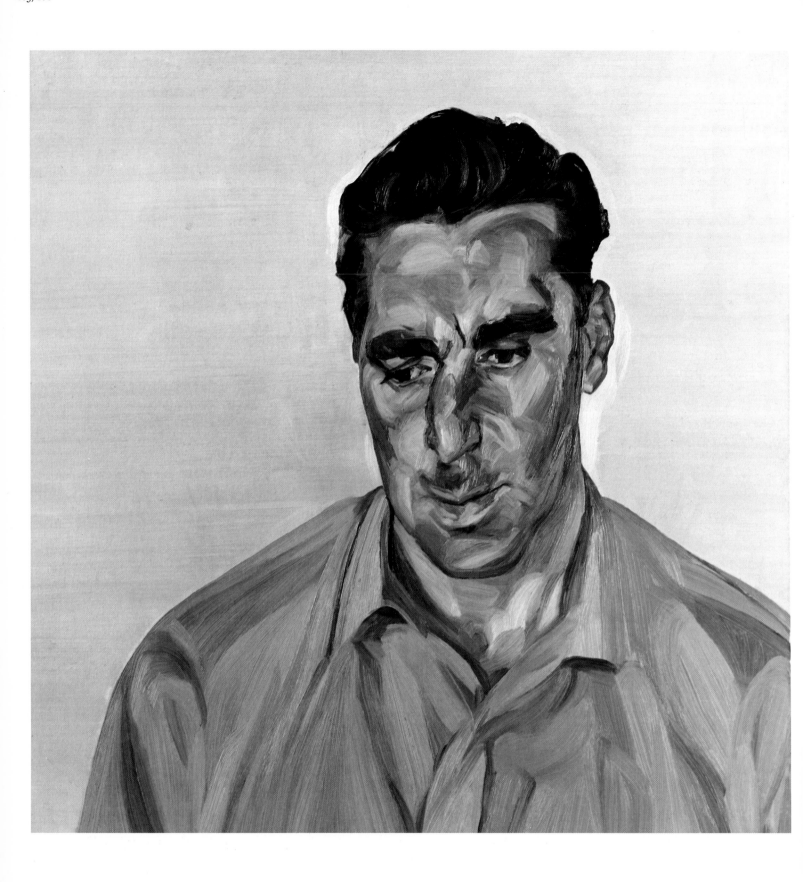

of zig-zag accents that manifest the principle of life which forms them are always to some extent inscrutable, never without the lively elusiveness of paint. Thinking of the metaphoric flatness of whatever is made with brush and colour, and the steady agreement with the plane, which is unexpected and uncovenanted in a style so fully and functionally modelled, thinking of this least-heralded among the graces of the painting that we know as figurative, I become aware that painting is figurative also in that other sense of a figure of speech. Referring to the transformation of figural solidity into paint, all the meanings of 'figurative' are the same.

After the fifteen and more years in which Freud had been invariably specific, definite and categorical, it does not seem that his purpose has changed. One cannot imagine that of him; he said lately, 'So far as I can remember I have always tried to do the same thing.' It is rather that *the definition*, the respect in which painting was definite, and equally the way in which it defined, suddenly became quite expansive; the *figure of paint* suddenly included meanings that it could never possibly have meant before. The sensuousness and the material richness, which Freud had set his face against as a youth, were suddenly at his disposal in altogether new forms, quite energetic, athletic even at their fattest, and with a constitutional imaginative spareness, quite different from the paint of the English post-Impressionists, which he had abjured as soon as he finished with the apples in Cedric Morris's stable. *Trying to do the same thing* must have meant determining on the enduring sense of painting, deciding that painting should always be in its entirety and every part identified as something physical and alive without the slightest doubt or escape, to the exclusion of non-sense, the cherished airs and graces and the concomitant mumbo jumbo. Or so I would guess. Freud's achievement at thirty may have convinced everyone but him. But the painter himself was on the move.

68   *Woman smiling* is listed as having been painted over a period of two years; I have heard Freud say 'I remember everything I've done because it was done with difficulty.' *Woman smiling*, as he told me, was the crucial picture in the unfolding of a greater fullness. It has been in his mind as I write, because he was painting the model again after twenty years. Like everything that happens in art, the change concerned (among other things) material and method. 'I had stopped drawing and worked with bigger brushes, hog-hair instead of sable.' The technical liberation was overtaken in the pictures that he went on to paint by transformations in every respect, in size and scale, in tempo and momentum, in subject and in the character of the paint itself. Shown a year or two later the new pictures were received with something like consternation: I remember thinking of the Russian patron who greeted the turning-point of modern painting with a lament for the loss to French art.

94, 95   The pictures that Freud began when he was forty were a drastic reversal of what was expected of him. Many of them were nearly twice life-size, and looked bigger; a powerful momentum ran through the paint, streaking it coarsely. The subjects were dynamically disoriented – tilted diagonally, leant backward or tipped in a corner. The sitter who figured most often appeared correspondingly uncompromising; she had a long face with a square chin and a fountain of hair which invited, if it did not suggest, the looping, arching brush-strokes that mark the pictures – mark them literally, groove the paint in the curving sweeps or the straight stripes of the unwavering brush-strokes. Illustration does these pictures no justice; on

(continued following plate 109)

the scale of the original the drawing is very complete and convinced, indeed lyrically involved in the distrait grace of the sitter. The brush comes sweeping down, zig-zagging across the canvas, encompassing the solidity as it loops to and fro. It describes great churning curves which make the form, recreate the pose and impulsively enact, as it seems, the expression. One feels in the paint how genial, how affectionate, the sitter was. Without the original one is at a loss to convey in the arms raised to the head, for example, a tremulous nervous strength.

The colour is as unexpected, broad and beautiful to match; anything rosy or evanescent in flesh vanishes to be replaced by the solid and lasting brick-red that appeared two or three years earlier in the second of the Chatsworth portraits. The same picture inaugurated the sweeping drawing that catches the shape whole in a network of boldly brushed alignments. Boldly brushed and yet consistently responsive and perceptive – finding and losing, then finding again, the axes of shape, temperament and expression together, and identifying for them the intimate colour, which a head secretes. From this time onwards a beautifully drawn head by Lucian Freud (there is hardly one that does not meet the prescription) shows the balance of asymmetries in which personality, emotion and private history recreate themselves before our eyes.

The reversal in 1960 is nevertheless startling; to love the pictures one must have in mind their place in the whole arch of Freud's development, and what they contributed to the vastly enriched resources of the paintings that followed them. Sitting for Freud lately, I asked him how it came about. He explained, 'My awareness that I wanted to work in a different way was fired by a period of unhappiness that made it impossible for me any longer to paint sitting down. You know how you can't sit down when you are unhappy? I was aware that my work wasn't a vehicle for my feelings ... No, that is not quite right. I didn't want my work to carry feeling in an expressionist way.' (He told me that Soutine disappointed him in 1963, 'Because I could see how it was done!') He went on, 'I had never questioned before that my way was the only way I could work. I saw there was something wrong about the distance between how I felt and the way I was working. I felt that I was doing *art work*.' His disgust was evident. 'I felt ... I'll just look out of the window.' It was hard to talk about and I needed no more. But a little more was in store. Coming from the house where we had been to look at the 1960 pictures, the violent momentum of the paint, from top to bottom of the big square canvases, still rushing in my head, I tried again. 'Were they a reaction against something?' The answer had some of the snaky venom. '*Everything* I do is a reaction against something!'

(continued following plate 121)

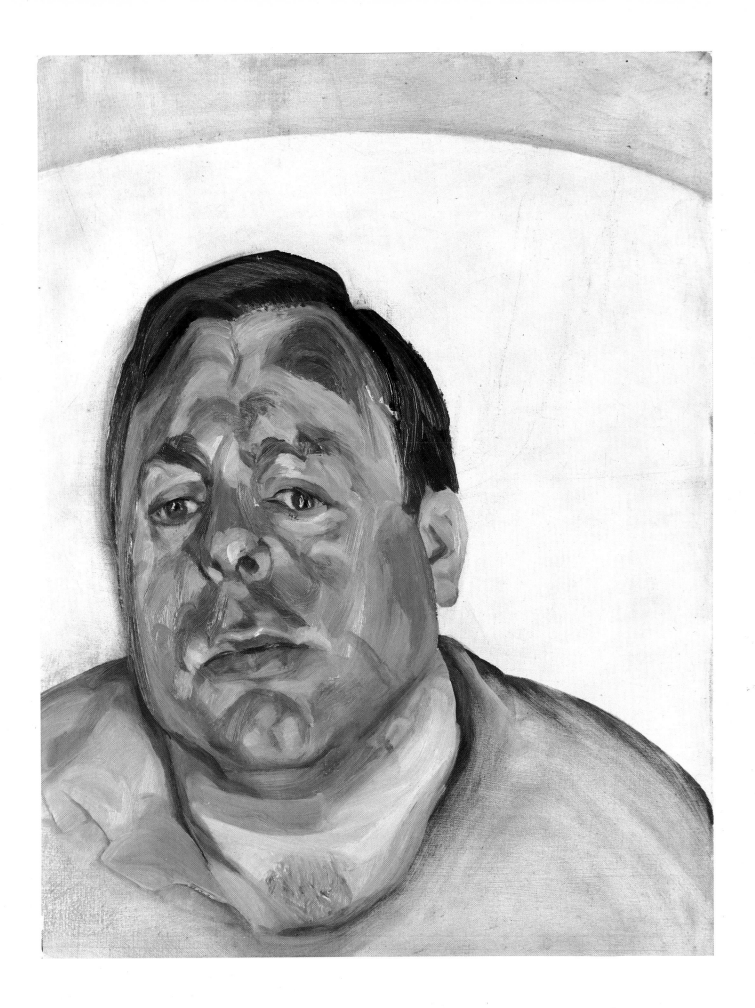

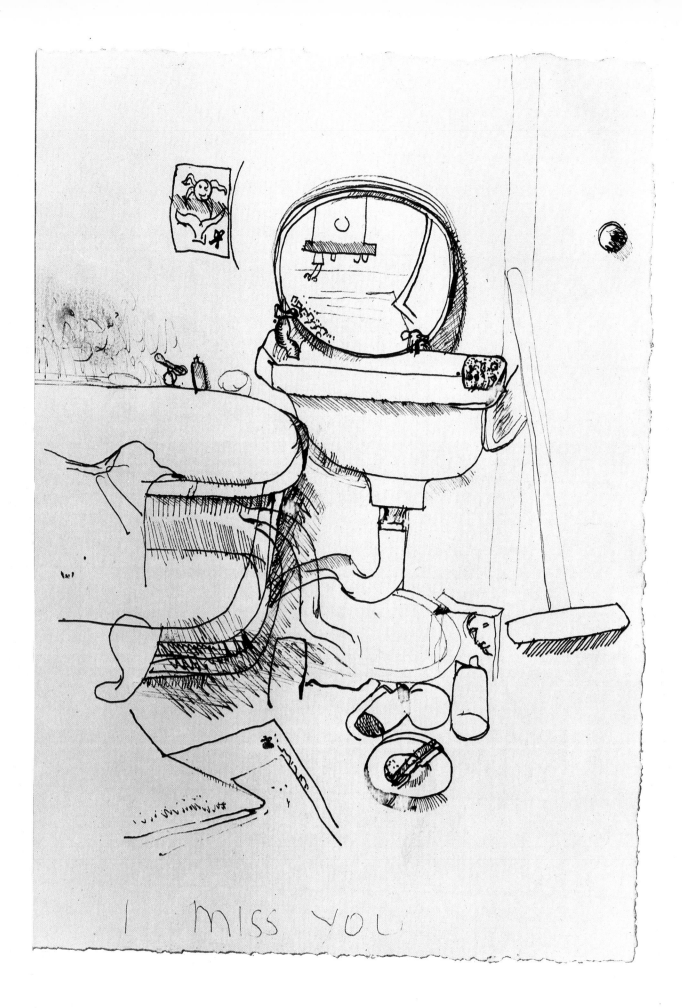

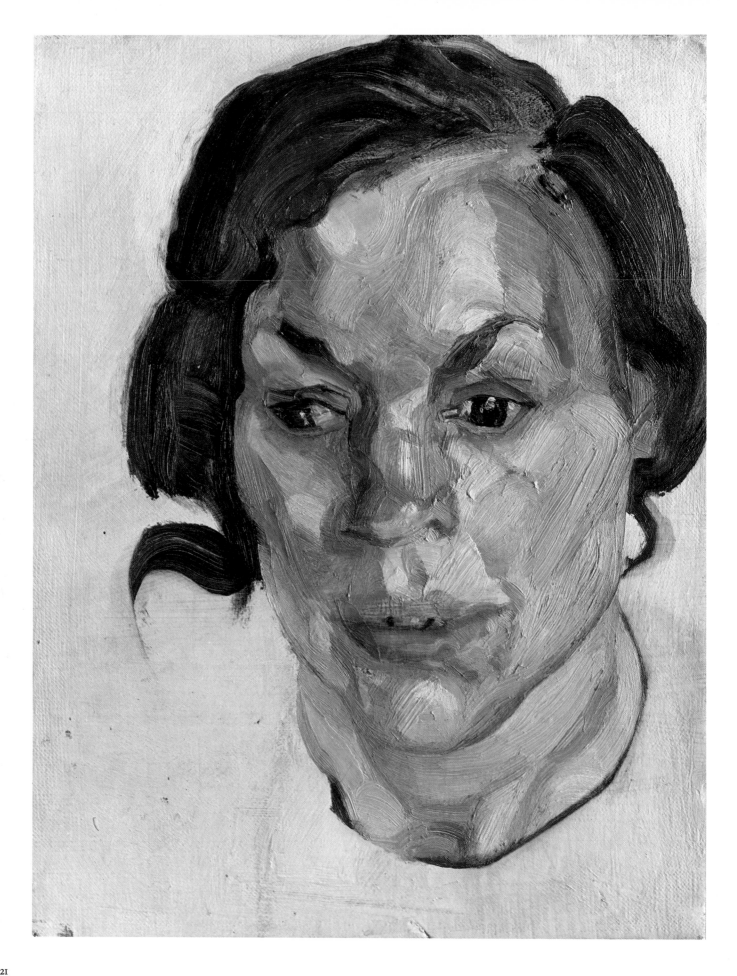

Standing to paint, Freud galvanized the 1960 pictures with an impetus that was altogether new. The room that he was working in was long and narrow. He painted big as if to combat its limitations. The scale of the pictures was a way of dealing with the proportions of the room. 'Do you know, if there is very little to eat it makes you terribly hungry?' The pictures are nothing like Bacon's. Yet giving up drawing it was in his mind that Bacon's urgency had to do with the fact that paint was his only means of expression. Bacon taught himself to draw with paint, which had never been done before.

But Freud yielded no ground to the romantic distortions of expressionism. Before I started writing he served me with notice of the fact. It was the day of his pronouncement against picture-making. As I edged into the studio, as heavy-footed as Freud is light, and wondered how to get a grip, there was another embargo, which eliminated one of my usual holds from this bout. 'I don't want to make painting look like the solving of a problem. I want it to be more inevitable than that.' He was quite firm on unhappiness. 'Eliot has something marvellous.' He fetched the book '"... The more perfect the artist, the more completely separate in him will be the man who suffers and the mind which creates." It really makes clear that art is a sort of filter.'

Yet looking back, turning over photographs of the pictures, we find that he has presided over a world of deep feeling. Not of effusive expression or eloquence, so much as a world in which states of being and shapes of being, the actual anatomy of human existence, possess their whole serious quality, and throw the condition of living open to the eye. Among the things that happened in 1960 and the years that followed, the most significant and lasting was perhaps the discovery that size, the actual scale of living form and the scale of its image are of their essence, bearing a relation to the actual dimension which is as much metaphoric or poetic as factual. I have the impression that metaphor is not one of the words that Freud likes best. At lunch, the very lunch at which the publisher of this book was led to the notion that it should be wrapped in leaves like some spicy delicacy, and the painter gathered that his name meant too much to us for us to imagine the book wrapped without it, although it matters not at all to him, indeed is felt to be as extraneous as it would be on his pictures ... at lunch, it was quite without knowing that such things had been in my mind and my manuscript that Freud leant forward and demanded, 'Why did Courbet call the *Atelier* an allegory?' He endured the lameness of my account for a moment or two before he broke in, with a sting in his impatience that was rather waspish than venomous, 'There was surely nothing metaphorical about Courbet's relations with his sisters!'

The scale (in every sense) of the 1960 pictures represented an expansion of the physical meaning of paint that painting was in urgent, crying need of. For a time, scale was seen as a token of physical presence. There is an unforgettable picture called *Sleeping head*, painted in the looping yellow streaks of the early sixties, above life-size, again, and plump to the point of grossness. The grossness of sleep, it seems; lying back, the fatness of neck and shoulder assumes its full value: eye and brush fondle the puppy-fat. The face recedes backward into darkness and recedes deeper now that some of the detail above it has been removed. At another look one finds the plumpness is not gross at all. It is rounded most delicately, lovingly;

97

the portrayal takes part in the dream. The sitter was never seen again; a casual meeting resulted in a picture that was finished in a week. Freud explained its character, 'I was going to do a nude, then I realized that I could do it from the head.' *Doing it* was capturing the substantive totality, the whole body, in paint. *Could* meant able to recognize the whole in the part, the rapture of sleep in the contentment, the whole silky richness of the body in the one conjunction of shoulder, neck and chin. This condensation of a nude was the beginning of a two-way traffic in awareness; the nudes of the next ten years, perhaps Freud's masterpieces, were expansions of the portrait.

The transporting scale of *Sleeping head* is inseparable from the image of somnolent rapture. Pictures like this enlarge the *figure of paint* (as one says, figure of speech), which has concerned Freud one way and another ever since. Scale is the indispensable surprise, the continuously necessary *reaction against something*, which is called on to enrich the essential subject, the human and bodily existence that paint stands for, the subject that engrosses him, as far as I have been able to notice, all the time. With attention one can gather from Freud's pictures, gather it directly from the paint, that life and love are for him in aid of painting, not the other way about. To gather the full subversive force of Freud's position, one needs to know that for him painting, which life and love are enlisted in aid of, is nothing more or less than making human shapes in paint. Not likenesses or effects or impressions or descriptions; not the light, except in one kind of picture reserved for it. Not distinctions or identifications or names and addresses or degrees of consanguinity. Just the visible, physical forms made in oil paint. A sense of the infinite implications, the necessity and the beauty of this finite operation can make a painter, when painting is in good shape, and that is how we find it now in one or two London studios. Chief among them, Lucian Freud's.

I was made aware of the surprises when Freud first asked me to a studio of his a few years ago. It was in Paddington; I was so accustomed to not knowing exactly where that I cannot now remember. There was no telephone number, as there still is not. As now on the stairs at – wherever it is – I am reminded, not at all inappropriately, of Picasso and the door of his apartment at rue de la Bóetie, with a grill placed so as to prevent a caller reaching the bell. I was not then conscious of the rarity of a request to call; I do not know how it came about, whether I had written or was to write, or simply that I was thought, how wrongly, to have seen the point. The surprise I was invited for must have been the picture that he was painting. I had been out of touch with what he was doing; in particular, I had not realized the part which sheer size was playing in his work and imagination; I use the word for the faculty that generates image art. So I was unprepared to be confronted by two pictures, not big, but inherently massive, gigantic in their imagining. Looking at them, as always with a new picture, perplexed – I am slower than a pen lets me appear; perplexed, but never, I admit, dumbfounded; perplexed, and I heartily mistrust anyone who is not, or the new painting that

145, 157 does not perplex him; particularly perplexed that day to hear Freud murmur *The big man*. He must have been trying the title out. Trying it for size. I was unprepared for exactly what is, in both senses, great about these pictures. The word never recovered from George Moore's account of its application to a landscape by B.W. Leader, but it is needed for Lucian Freud's pictures of bigness, far more than for the vaster canvases of his time. These pictures are about bigness and manhood in equal proportion. Both the size of the man and the adult figure he cuts are intimidating. I remember the embarrassment of that reversal of expectations, which I no longer separate from the extension of experience in art. The amplitude of his social bulk and its evident acceptability to people who never reckoned much to artists, except as men who have nude models in their studios, are impressive; I am sentimental about the stature of the big man in a dimension that is closed to me, as Rembrandt was sentimental about rabbis. I happen to know that the big man owns betting shops, but the pictures would permit an equivalent impression on grounds of formal coherence and harmony of aspect alone. Find me another sitter in a portrait who musters a bulk, an unassuming, effortless compactness, an integration that compare with this, and I will show you as good a painter as Lucian Freud; they come no better. Painting is not made more life-shaped than this.

It may be that the reversal of expectations is central to the signification of the art that we know as modern, as it surely is to music, with its necessity, in every phrase and sequence that is meaningful, of an interval that is just not, precisely and measurably not, the interval that was foreseen. It is a question what part of this order of meanings is at root social, geared, that is to say, as much to the status of the expectation as the quality of its rebuttal. In painting, where the transmitted expectation affects not only the picture but the persona of the painter, where style is the convention of how the painter-man behaves, even the convention that he behaves and paints surprisingly, the patterns of behaviour that the painter accepts or rejects, even the social figure that he cuts, is never unconnected with his creation. Painting now, there is just one artist among those whose consecrated modernity is undoubted, whose reversal of expectations concerns only the surprise of what is real – Lucian Freud. No one understands better than he that, if art is what the artist does (and the only problem is to guess to whom it applies), then the converse is equally well established. It was in this context, on my first visit to the Paddington studio, where I saw the canvases of *The big man* and numbly failed to cope with the surprise, that Freud stood in the painting room as if abstractedly, but with the trace of formality that I now recognize, with which something or other is to be mentioned *once*, and the look of solicitude with which it will be mentioned to someone who appears talkative rather than attentive, mentioned therefore at dictation speed. I had referred vaguely to his home or family; an expectation required reversing. Freud announced, 'I have always kept my studio.' The expectation of domesticity is rooted in me. 'Wives and children?' I had no idea what my question involved, but I understood that it had arisen to some extent or other. 'I could always come back to the studio at night.' The communication had been made and I appreciated it, because I was immediately aware that my expectation, uncorrected, would have falsified paintings that I knew and was to know, in respects that I am trying to account for to this day. My cosy expectation tampered with a persona that was thought of as inseparable from them.

Thinking back to the rooms at Paddington, all more or less painting rooms, I return to the brass bedstead under the painting lights, the most magnificent brass bedstead one could buy. It was evidently what a property master lists as a practical bed, and not in its first freshness. Freud's own manner of life is fastidious, and latterly rather grand. Painting, he studies to the limit the milieu of the unmade bed.

Among the pictures at the studio, I remember another surprise. The paint was thick and clotted in little lumps, thicker than any pictures of Freud's I had seen – for a painter uncomfortably, embarrassingly thick, the kind of paint that the rest of us think it impossible to work over. It took me a year or two to realize that embarrassment was his ally. Painting, he is in alliance with the gross material of the paint, just as he is in alliance with the physicality and the body of his model. Treated his way, with robust appreciation and without caution, they are indeed life-long allies; they make pictures.

The best of Freud's pictures, those of the last twenty-five years, the years of the expansion that began with *Woman smiling*, represent such a transformation as only comes to a painter brave and proud and bored enough never to copy himself. These pictures are only truly comprehensible and beautiful in the context of their milieu. I distinguish it from the milieus

68

and habits of his peers in the School of London, few of them any more regular, but all of them different. Each follows a distinct conception of how a Man Painter, a painter-man, behaves. (The title of *A woman painter* still irks me.) For each a different persona, a different culture. Freud's pictures could not have come out of the milieu and culture of domesticity.

In these last twenty years Freud has painted people with incomparable positiveness and confidence. At Chatsworth, the head of the family, failing a portrait of his daughter, whom Freud did not feel he could paint, commissioned one of his mother, the third of Freud's pictures for the house. At first sight the drawing appears almost summary. Yet it is evidently just this directness which allows such precision in establishing the elderly dignity and poise. Again, a habitual turn of the head is full of personal history; it conveys the element of amused tolerance in a lifelong understanding of her own. Though the touch seems blunt the sharpness of a nostril is defined with a unique deftness, which is quite without bravura; it only follows the form with evident and selfless respect.

The category of *good portrait* (as laudably inoffensive as *good conduct*) is a usual and comfortable idea. We have to relinquish the notion, of which it is a measure of talent to disabuse us, that sitters are all alike and painters all much the same. If character and behaviour were continually fresh and unforeseen, we could expect that the visible response to them, personally wrought in accordance with the same irregular amalgam of communicable reason and strangeness, would be unlike any other artefact of man. We might predict that it would impress us in respects both profound and irresistible, as does our deepest knowledge of our kind. So it turns out to be with great portrait-painting. If we can abandon our assumption that we are looking at a quite usual thing, we shall find ourselves in the presence of something unparalleled and wonderful. If we recognize novelty and wonder in such experiences, and take the chance to isolate and savour a sense of what is intimate and unintended in people, we shall come to cherish these images as much as anything we know.

With Freud one cannot help noticing that, as he became both more thoroughly engrossed in how people really are and still more dexterous at his craft, he became not more foreseeable or conventional, but more responsive to the genuine, unwilled oddness that human nature and capacity, left to fulfil themselves, do not conceal. He had, and has now more than ever, a sensible talent for abstaining from rationalization, and he naturally detects a talent for naturalness in others. The sitter for the third Chatsworth picture, with the title *Portrait of a woman*, exceptionally unindicative even for him, but not overweening in its demand that the particular should be judged by its universality, asked him, 'Why are you so interested in my family?' The question left Freud mildly surprised that people in any category, even a family, should be regarded collectively. For him they were individuals who happened to be related, and it was as such that he painted them, as he paints anyone. Certainly, to engage Freud to this extent was a sign in itself of an imaginative calibre likely to be more than interesting. We get a glimpse of the kind of patron and the kind of involvement that Freud attracts in the portrait of his sitter's son, painted a couple of years later, which faces hers in this book. It was, in the unforced way that Freud's pictures are, a crucial step.

(continued following plate 127)

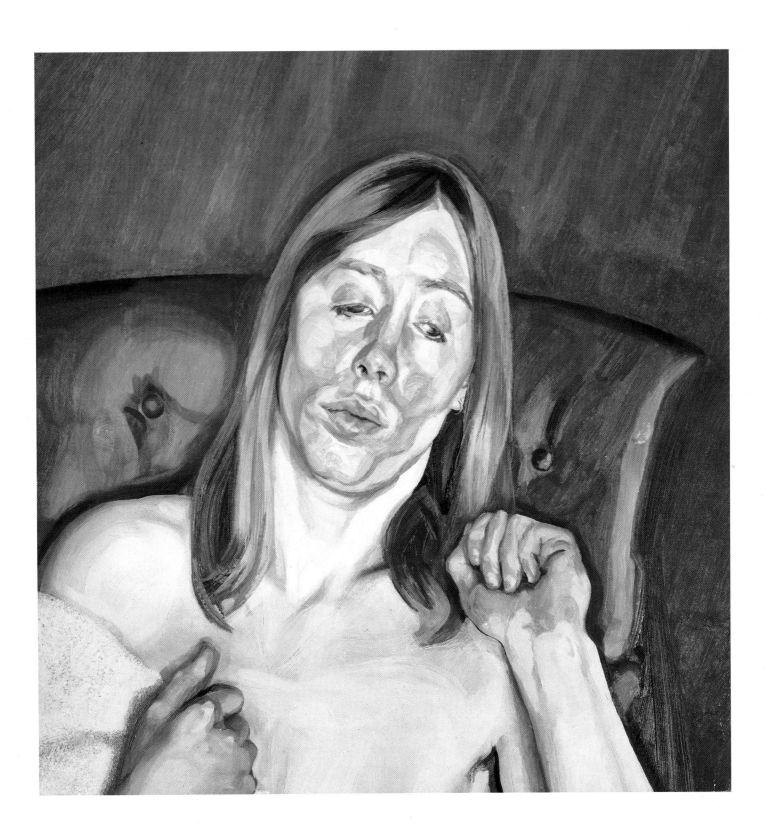

125, 126, 127

It was already clear that Freud had no intention of regarding the relief of a head as a normal occasion for perfunctory modelling. The extraordinary incidence of protruberance and hollow surprises him each time. His brush chases back and forth and up and down. Every forehead, every temple is exceptional; a fresh and different urgency drives him each time. In this series the fourth Chatsworth portrait was a dramatic and extreme development. At first one supposes that the top of the canvas had a brown priming. Underlying the oyster-grey there is a foxy colour that re-emerges in the modelling of the forehead. At the bulge of the dome, thin paint laid across stiff paint loses some of its legibility and continuity to the obtrusive square brush-strokes underneath. It is the kind of eventuality that painters fear and when I saw the picture I was, as usual, mystified. But it was, in a double sense, a break-through. Several kinds of history were being quite consciously superimposed.

'Awareness of mortality', Freud told me, 'made me leave a corner of the underpainting blank.' And then, 'He was in an alcoholic phase. There were marvellous patches of mauve and yellow round his cheeks, which helped me a lot.'

All the time, a painter like this is gathering strength. Freud's athletic stamina had been linked to a growing sense of painting in time, painting as narrative, painting in his model's life and in his own and most of all to painting as the image of mortality. He likes to recall the remark of the painter in Henry James' *The Tragic Muse* to a pretentious young man who is sitting to him, 'I wonder what you will do when you are old.' The sitter never comes again. 'That is one of the things you think of when you are working from someone.' He has an acute sense of what to do to ensure that painting keeps pace with the changes in him as the years pass. He does not wear spectacles to paint; 'If you want to keep on I think it is best not to.' When his father died in 1970 after depositing something in Freud's imaginative resource, which has been increasingly understood, with the treasured portfolio of watercolours in the studio drawer, he began on a series of portraits of his mother.

The portraits were now moulded more and more as life moulds flesh. As the conception of surface continuity ceased to govern him, the breaches of consistency became increasingly abrupt and meaningful. It is partly due to the fourth Chatsworth picture that he has been able, in portraits like *Frank Auerbach*, to put more of the human forehead into pictures than you could gather in the whole previous history of painting.

162

There is nothing particularly artistic or stylish about this. Yet the moist way the bulges glisten in the light, so that the greasy lustre, which is inseparable from real skin, tells so truly the actual shape and the personal urgency behind it – this grips our attention as only the finest does in any art. And where the skin does not shine, where its own opalescent brown-pink warmth rounds the shape down into the creases formed by habit, endurance and love – there we are reminded over again that none of the reasons for art compare in their hold on us with the straightforward human reasons. There is no getting away from it; the skin is indisputably modelled by the pressure inside it, making the shape that is so uniquely complex and yet so natural – the kind of shape that we truly recognize, and have feelings for.

(continued following plate 141)

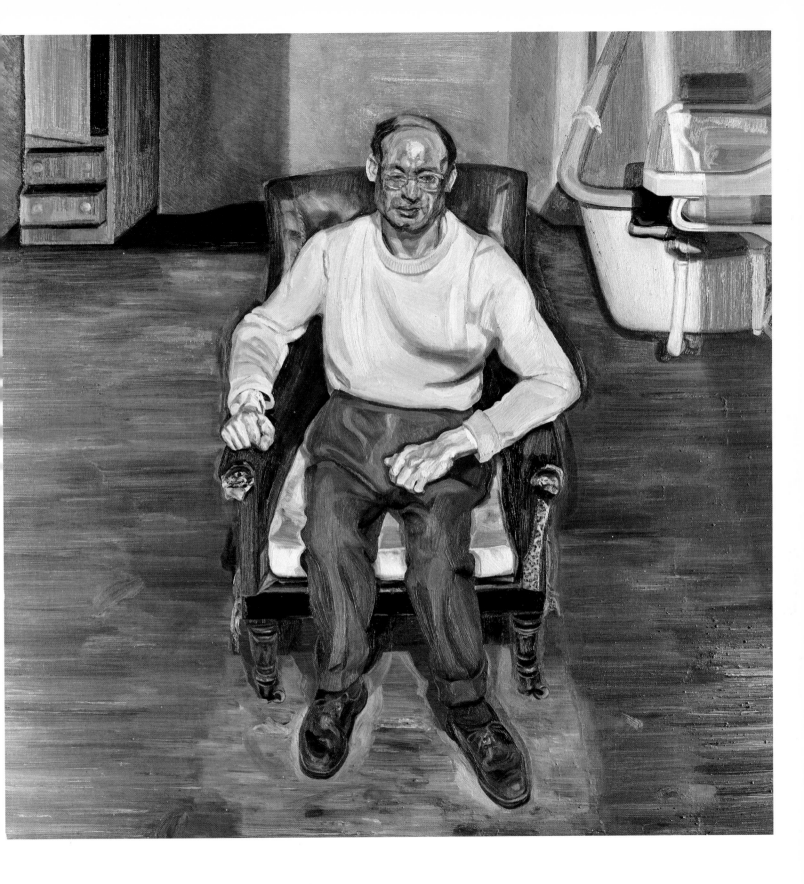

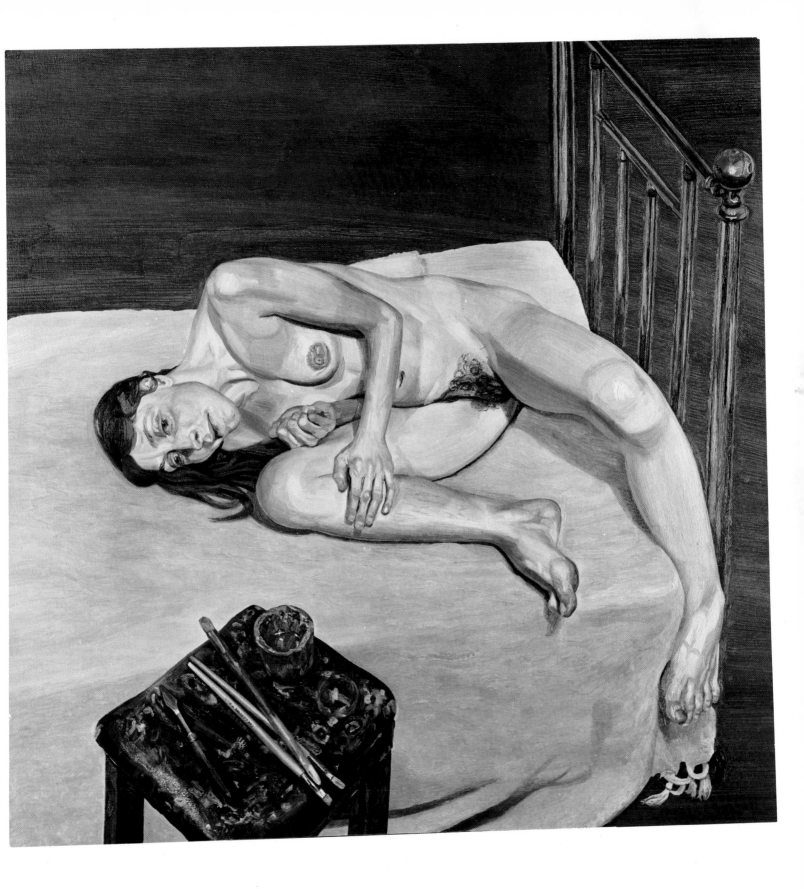

Between family, friends and the occasional patron who engages his interest, Freud seems to have painted the whole range and compass of personality in the last twenty years. There is the impulsive temperament and pronounced features that inspired the headlong rush of 1960. There is the complex, sensitive sitter for two portraits, whose head turned a little, at an angle both attentive and reflective, as if she were hearing distant music. In one portrait of his daughter Annabel he painted the innocence of affliction, with heartbreaking sweetness; four years later he showed the tragic confusion. The profound diffidence of a Soho friend, hunched in his soiled gaberdine, with a downcast, inward look like grief, was eventually realized, above life-size, as a talent in itself and painted with the arching brush strokes of the sixties. A lovely sitter with hollow cheeks and long fair hair, whom he painted often, had slightly pursed lips, as if whistling an Irish air. The individuation, the distinctness of each, make it a splendid array. Freud remembers another of Wittgenstein's remarks; 'It is already rare to be a person.'

The fact that these sitters are thoroughly themselves, their own people and no one else's, is at the heart of these pictures. The canvases were more and more often square; they contain themselves naturally like people do. The sitters may own one another's pictures; they sometimes seem like a club, or a union for mutual knowledge, on behalf of painting that is inseparable from lives and relationships. Painting for Freud is still connected with gathering things and people he likes, particular ones that remain obstinately themselves. His stepson Kai, whom naturally he was painting, found a banana suit, a zipped yellow overall complete with stalk, and Freud, who immediately wanted one, had to explain to the shopman seeking his specifications: 'I want *your* banana suit, not *my* banana suit.'

One kind of portrait has been, as it always is, essentially apart. 'The information gathered from a mirror', he told me at the start, 'is a very different kind of information.' Then, when I pressed him a week or two later, he seemed at a loss: 'I think it is the light.' So it comes about that the self-portraits are like a tribute to an opposite order of painting. The physical presence, the immediacy, the probing, the things collected from over the optical horizon in case he finds a use for them, have no place. Instead, in the later self-portraits there is only the grey mirage within the imagined zone of a mirror, the flat wafer of specifically and solely visual awareness.

He used to leave the mirror lying about, trying it continually in different places. In *Interior with plant, reflection listening* the distance to the glass between the leaves of a great plant yields a memorable image of solitariness. The dynamic action and reaction of the square-brushed paint were the theme of the tiny pictures called *Man's head* in 1963. Four years later, *Interior with hand mirror* was an essay in the involved inversions of contre jour. He painted his model of the time nude against the light, with Daumier's washerwomen in mind, and disliked the result. In the mirror on the window the eyes are screwed up against the light; he is looking in some sense against the grain. The whole face is clenched, yet not with the effort of it, so much as a debonair habit, shrugging the personal involvement off, a minute convulsion like shyness, which receives the light on the bridge of the nose and cheek-bone. The earlier miniature self-portrait, with a finger between the lips, has a confessional quality. He has no time for the light;

(continued following plate 153)

117

100, 101

132

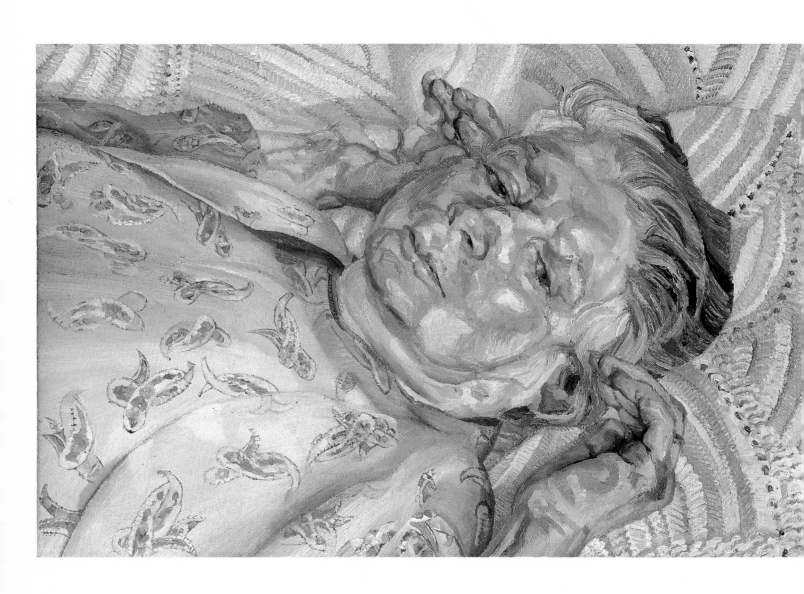

143, 144

145, 146

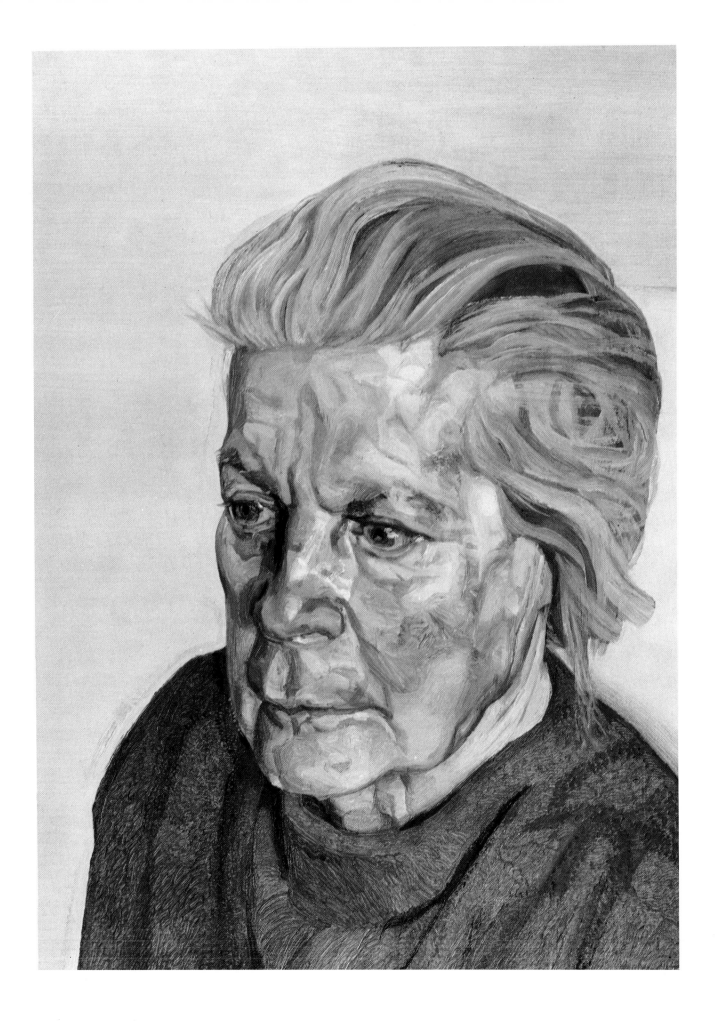

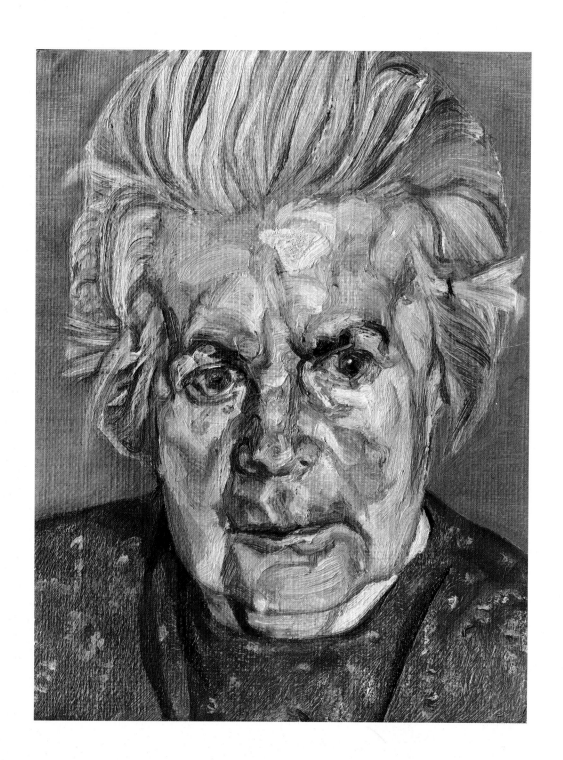

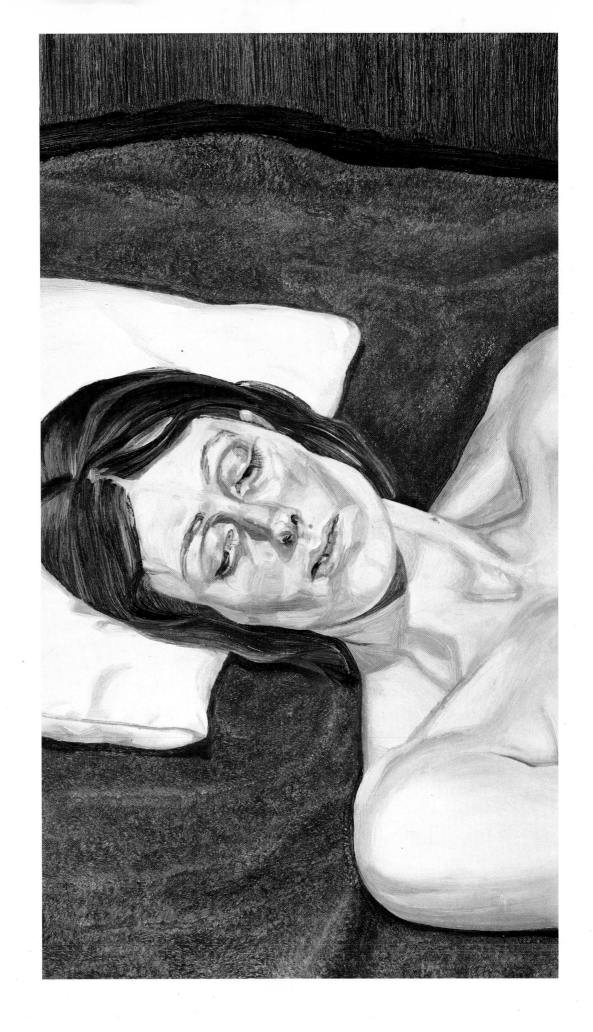

he is feeling inside himself. The self-portrait with a thistle in the Tate is without this quality. Lucian told me, 'When I saw it again it annoyed me. I don't know why.' It does not appear in this book.

The self-awareness of these tiny pictures was the awareness of a provisional alternative. Freud's view of anything but himself has never to this day been in the least like a mirage. One exceptional picture puzzles his admirers, *Reflection with two children*. It studies directly the zone of illusion, investigates whether its contents could be given monumental status like sculpture, examines if the visual package could be made solid in itself, so that another image of unrelated scale might be propped against it, like a cut-out snapshot on a mirror frame, or … the two children carved on the plinth of a sculpture of the dwarf Seneb in the Cairo Museum. The Vienna edition of Breasted's *History of Egypt*, a present from his father years ago, which is always in his studio, usually open at the heads from Amarna, bore fruit at last. Whether the result of any of these experiments was positive is still not quite certain. The Egyptian fidelity and reserve appear by contrast enduringly stoic. *107, 108, 109*

There have been occasional signs of proneness to a self-image of defiant isolation, bony, even dwarfish in the raking light. It is the only part of his work in which his enormous mastery seems as if manipulated to fortify a posture that is defensive, with latent tones of hostility and sorrow. The possibility of them is moving; the warmth and the eventual sensuous sweetness of the other, outgoing aspect, nourished by and nourishing the rest of his work, gains a sharp resonance from this momentary hint of the reverse. The information gathered from a mirror is certainly a different kind of information.

The subjects themselves explain that it is studio life which makes pictures. It is bodily life, living and painting for real, with no holds barred. Under a big studio tree – Freud is never without some such indoor landscape to this day – a child sleeps naked in the biggest picture that he attempted till quite lately. The same scene observed in a mirror includes the painter at work on it. It gives the single glimpse of his lunging, swaying gait across a studio floor. The real painter-man is quite unlike the obsessive phantom of *Reflection with two children*. *131 130*

At about the same time the sitter with the pursed lips and silky hair inspired the remarkable enlargement of portraiture. Freud explained, 'It is interesting to try to portray them *completely*.' He looked down on the naked girls sprawled on the floor – from a god-like standpoint, as Jupiter in the guise of a satyr saw Correggio's *Antiope*. At first there is something gaunt about the body, spread-eagled at midnight under the light-bulb and the painter's eye. The light and the scrutiny washed the softening transitions away, leaving unhidden the angular awkwardness of limbs and the indomitable lumpiness, with which the body-shape is modelled by the life inside it. *125, 126, 122*

The next group revolves round the sitter with the heavy-lidded eyes. The completeness of this portraiture extends to what is unseen, both the private recesses of physical life and its particular frames of mind. One picture is a veritable icon of on-edge-ness. The poses become eloquent of the tension and the suspense of the night, as well as the abandonment. In the latest of the naked portraits nothing of the richness of a body is lacking. Freud has painted its constitution, its contents, its community, its congress. Portraying *Pregnant nude* he finds *138*

159

analogy that is a painterly allegory. The pregnancy, which has run full-term, culminates in a ripeness with the veinous bloom of some great fruit, which is more *painted* than any other gamut of shot and broken colour in Freud's work, and not only painted, but spread across the canvas in illuminating chromatic company with the red and green threads of the sofa and its *158,* contents, frayed, worn-through and coming apart. In *Naked girl with egg* the analogy and the accord of colour are even plainer.

The milieu and culture of the studio are more vivid than ever in the recent pictures. There is certainly nothing allegorical about the splendid presence in paint which makes the latest nudes work as flesh works. The grandest of them bear the names of daughters. If the male counterparts are companionably rat-like, that community of feeling is accommodated too. Everything is physical; it is fully defined and definite. *The figure of paint*, as I call it, is the committing, self-forgetful working of a living image in pigment. If we follow the sublimation we shall call it sublime. It is figurative in every respect. The centre of gravity in Freud's recent painting is not the illustration or the fantasy. It is the simple quality of representation, which anyone can see, the fact that the human subject is better made, more 'living and precise' and more seriously realized than any other painter is capable of.

Anyone can see it; the truism is unquestioned. What is open to debate is the critical proposition, that virtue and value in painting are connected with its status as admirable figurative craftsmanship, like an object of virtù. Luckily painting as good as this does not need critical debate. Having climbed the critical ladder, we throw it away; the philosopher is surely in mind. Kick it away, I would guess. All we need is to recognize that the elusive emotional colouration, the dark as well as the light of a man, could not have emerged except in the metaphor of paint moulded visually and manually on outward experience, with the exceptional compulsion, an emotional drive that is, perhaps unusually, powerful, and a realism to match it.

The loaded paint that first surprised me on my visit to the Paddington studio grew heavier and more encrusted. It coagulated in little lumps which accumulated more of the drying paint, until the surface was coarsely granular where he had always needed it to be most refined. He explained that this was caused by Kremnitz White, a pigment with twice as much lead even as Flake White; he handed me a tube to feel its weight. Often he painted on regardless; sometimes he scraped it flat as the rest of us would have done. He always finishes by getting a unique and luminous consistency of his own. In *Pregnant nude*, for example, the light itself seems to granulate as it falls on the thighs, with an incandescence that is very responsive to the richness of flesh. 'I quite like flesh having Kremnitz White as a Leitmotif, but then I am afraid of losing unity and adopt it for hair and clothes as well.' Watching the new picture, which is the biggest picture that he has attempted, I found myself brooding on the lumps and spots and fearful of the risk to the equation of flesh with paint which I enjoy. Half the usefulness of Kremnitz White was perhaps that it prevented the kind of painting that people wanted him to go on doing. 'When you talk about the equation,' he said, 'It makes me uneasy. I want paint to *work as flesh*, which is something different. I have always had a scorn for "la belle peinture" and "la delicatesse des touches". I know my idea of portraiture came from dissatisfaction with portraits that resembled people. I would wish my portraits to be *of* the people, not *like* them.

Not having a look of the sitter, *being* them. I didn't want to get just a likeness like a mimic, but to *portray* them, like an actor.' (*Portray* was said with a peculiar intensity.) 'As far as I am concerned the paint *is* the person. I want it to work for me just as flesh does.'

The paint that constitutes his mother in the portraits of Lucie Freud works like this. It is more than three hundred years since a painter showed as directly and visually as much as his relationship with his own mother, and that was Rembrandt. The comparison is not incongruous. Few artists in any medium have admitted us to a relationship so intimate and so

(continued following plate 160)

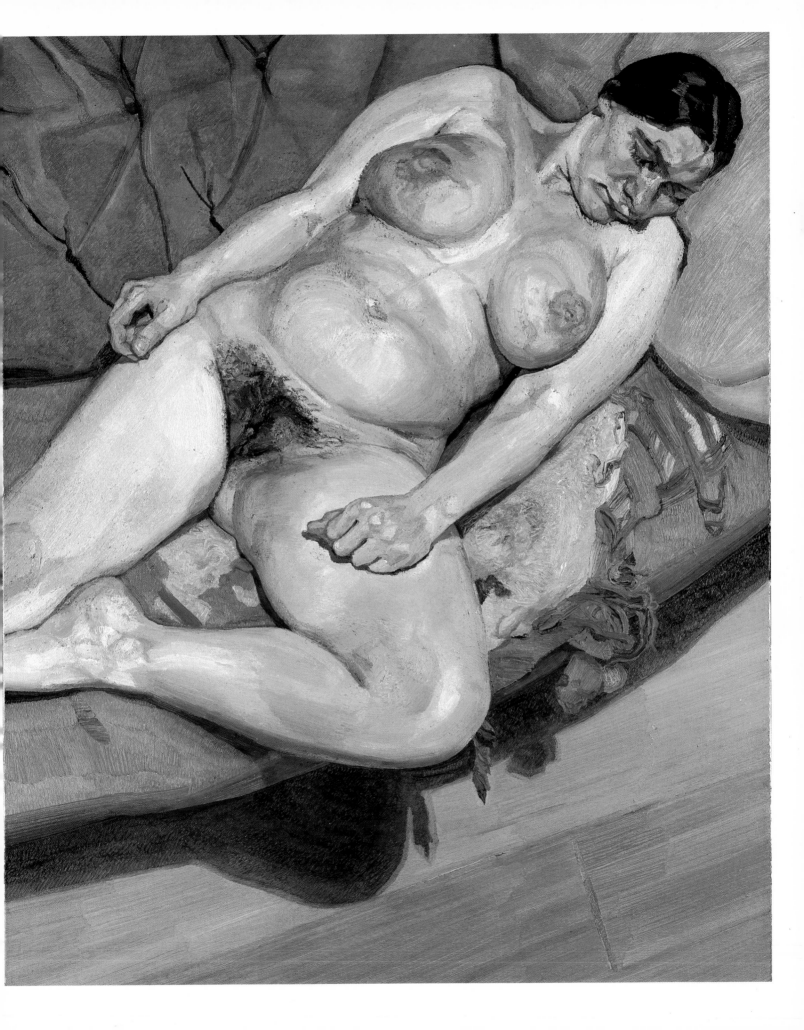

cherished. Freud began with concentrated canvases much smaller than the illustrations in this book. They are in every way pictures of concentration – the intense gathering of purpose in the head and the attentiveness of the painter, which is as concentrated as if he was taking dictation from the knotted muscle of the head. After four repetitions in the same year the whole complexity of shape and preoccupation was at last sorted out and realized. In later pictures the sitter is lying on a bed. She is resting, bathing contentedly in the relationship, in which affection is no more than the starting point for mutual comprehension, deepening respect and a closeness that is both affinity and sheer physical proximity, the sense of each other's bodily presence which is the recurring theme of figure painting. In one of the reclining pictures the mother rolls back like a baby or a kitten (or an odalisque by Matisse) as if remembering her child.

143

In another version it seems that an idol has reverently been laid flat for packing as a treasured masterpiece. The picture records the moment at which devotion dissolves into the extraordinary feeling, combining identification and detachment which we recognize as the emotion of art. The reference in these pictures is physical and material through and through. The colour has the density and texture of actual stuff. The paint itself is tufted like the bedspread, satiny like the cushion, and in the flesh it is impulsive yet constant, just as a person is. To make painting like people in ways that it was never like them before may not be the most severe of imaginative triumphs, but it is in a mysterious way incontrovertible. Listening now to Lucian's memories, I realize that we know a little how it was that by his eleventh year, when the family came to England, Lucian was drawing all the time. In the years before, he said, 'There was something I didn't tell you. About my mother. It was just that she used to make me give her drawing lessons.' Lucie Freud's face shows the calibre of the support that Lucian could count on from the woman whose name he bears. We need look no further for the source of his confidence, for the emotional return that art affords him and for the magisterial overtones that work in art with a woman always possesses. This wonderful woman has coloured Freud's whole life-work and this book.

164

Lucie Freud takes part in the last, so far, of her son's dramas-without-themes, and by far the most suggestive. In *Large interior, W.9.* the old lady sits musing in the foreground. On the floor by her chair there is a mortar with a judicious amount of newly-ground grey paint splashed about in it: it may be the same grey paint which has been brushed freely and impatiently onto the smooth canvas for her grey woollen dress. It is as if her son's splendid technical resource had been laid at her feet for her to reflect on. Behind her, across the width of the canvas, there is a nude girl on a bed, with a blanket over her legs. It is the girl with the heavy-lidded eyes who posed for the small naked portraits. There is a disproportion about the figure; it is said that it required more than twenty repaintings before its scale was established. (Freud does not remember.) She still does not quite recede, and should not; it is rather as if she existed in the dreams of the old lady between us, who is isolated in a world of her own, a darker pool. The girl is possessed by visionary idealism. In fantasy, at least, she has been admitted to the communion of mother and son. If it is imaginary, it is none the less sensual and sacred both at once, and she knows it. She looks up at the ceiling, flushed and wrapt,

134

(continued following plate 162)

58, 159, 160

161, 162

erotically excited and erect. A visionary experience of sexuality is being shared. One loves each figure through the other's eyes, with no holds barred, in attitudes that are unaccustomed. The experience is intense and it places *Large interior, W.9.* among the modern paintings that rank recognizably with the unaccountable in the art of any time. Freud has spoken about the images of the past which are 'so powerful that one cannot imagine how anyone could have made them or how they could ever not have existed.' That is how one feels about *Large interior, W.9.*

The pictures of studio life are always the biggest. Freud described how the latest, the biggest he has painted, came about. The owner of a great collection gave him a catalogue and in it Freud found a Watteau music party, which struck him. 'I intended first to make a copy of it. Then I thought, why don't I do one of my own?' What was astonishing was that the canvas on the easel measured more than two metres in both directions. He had lately painted the largest of his plant pictures, the one in the Tate, *Two plants*, 1977–80, in which the innumerable leaves have an almost physiognomic life in common, making faces together. He

134

160

had told me that the labour was intended to break in the new studio and populate the room. He must have thought of collecting things he liked, in his habitual way, on a larger scale still. At first Watteau seems surprising. Watteau's paintings were really about his drawings, which were for him the greater pleasure, and his drawings were about the life of the studio. His subject was his mercurial vision of his friends from the Comedies, sitting about to enjoy one another and be drawn, or passing amorously together to and fro. It is all encapsulated with silky lustre in the paint and the mise-en-scène.

It was not so incongruous that Watteau should have come to mind in connection with Freud's studio life. The diversions and the passion are the same; the style is different but fancy dress would not have made the genital drive any less imperative. To understand Watteau, or Keats, I used to think that one must have been host to tubercle, before antibiotics removed one more source of passion from those we can share. But no doubt a well-endowed drive more than matches pathology. I thought of the excitement of ruched silk when with Freud it was a matter of the tactile awareness excited by the soiled puckering of a gaberdine raincoat.

Re-imagining the Watteau subject, Freud recruited four or five of his favourite people. His daughter Bella, whom I knew from her pictures, played the mandoline; Kai, of the banana

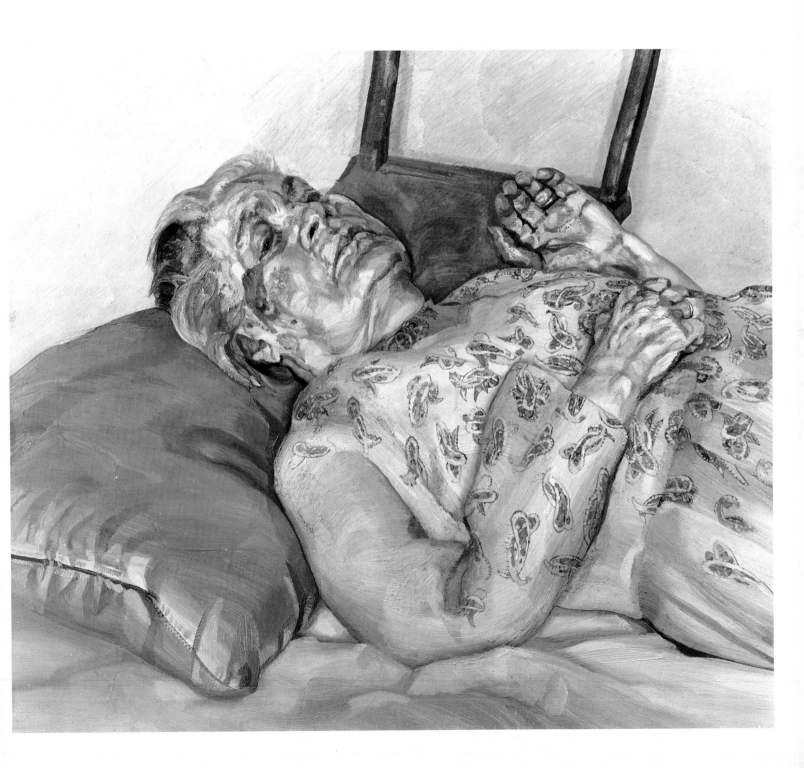

suit, took the part of Gilles. On either side, in the listeners, wearing corn-coloured silk dresses with flowers, fancy enough to recall the prototype, one recognizes the model for *Naked girl with egg* and, after twenty years, the sitter for *Woman smiling*. The expressions, which one now knows well and reads with pleasure, are enough to confirm that they *mean something*. For us the meaning is carried by the substance of its incarnation in paint. As I write, each is resolving in the painter's hands, and each in its own way. No consistency matters but the consistent and telling dictation from the forms of life. The younger is resolving serenely, with a delicate sadness that agrees with Watteau, the elder richly, with the same attention to the way little shapes, little muscles like strokes of colour, come together to compose not only the form but the life of a face, which must remind us of the great painter of older women. The question of how tradition comes to life in a painter is endlessly fascinating, and never more than in Freud who is in great part oblivious of it. Not entirely; I could have sworn that Correggio's *Antiope* returned, with exquisite appropriateness, as an involuntary memory. But I was wrong. Remembering Freud's *Cyclamen* I thought that Caravaggio's *Basket of fruit*, indeed the whole persona of the notorious seducer of the Piazza Navona, with his cult of life-painting and the valenthuomo, would have been in his mind, until I found that he was not so much aware of Caravaggio's separate existence. The echoes of Rembrandt mean most, because they evoke precisely what is most inimitable in him; they isolate exactly what one has in mind when one thinks of what is permanently and undeniably modern in Rembrandt, and constant in Freud, the same in *Woman smiling* twenty-three years ago as today. Without an interpreter, it is quite hard to describe the definition of Rembrandt, which makes his statement entirely physical and definite.

Freud works at night; my appointment to be drawn on his etching plate was at dawn. In winter the assignment is not too demanding, but I took pride in it, though I failed to control my eagerness to talk while I sat. The studio has a top-floor airiness. Sitting, I looked up at the coving of the ceiling and wondered how Freud would paint the belt of shadow and the light without the expedient of a mirror.

Another day he had been painting on the music party. The subject had unrolled a few more inches down the canvas by the time I arrived to discuss the book. Bella, who had been sitting, produced tea. Freud read Christian von Morgenstern to me in the salon of the apartment, which is a little formal and grand in a Viennese way. As I had no knowledge of his life and did not feel the need of it, we agreed to let the inquisitive molecules pester one another. Then Freud was speaking at dictation speed: '... There is another reason for not talking about my life. *It is still going on.*

Bella had finished; there were quiet transactions in the hall and the complex unlocking. Father and daughter went to the stairhead. Without listening I heard the lowered voices.

'I will see you at dawn then.'

'Definitely.'

166, 167, 168, 169

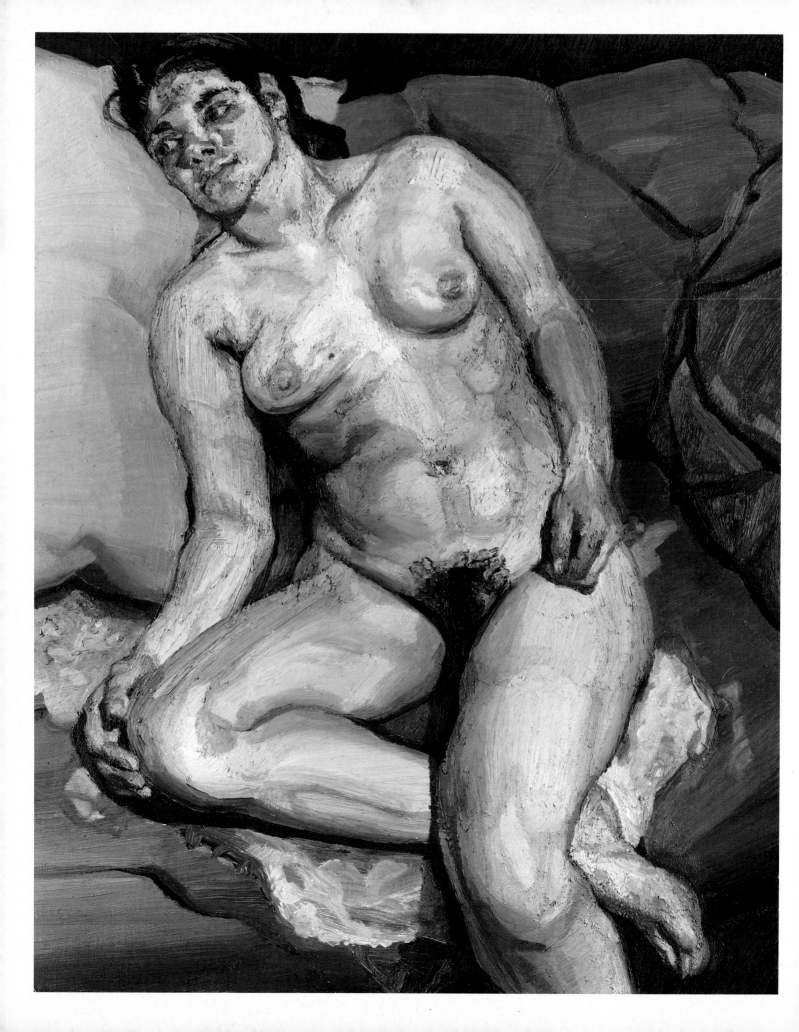

174, 175, 176, 177

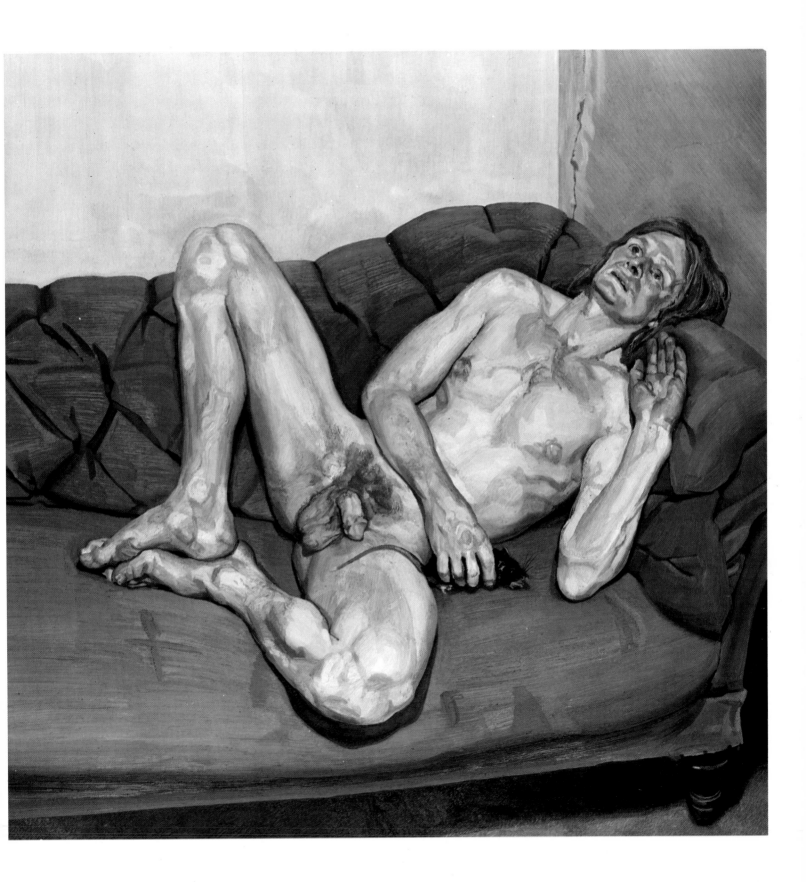

List of illustrations

All pictures are in private collections except where indicated. Measurements are given in inches and centimetres, height before width.

The following drawings, listed by page number, are reproduced in the text:

9 A couple, 1937
Brush and ink, 13½ × 10 in/34.3 × 25.4 cm

16 Stephen Spender, 1940
Brush and ink, 8⅜ × 5¾ in/21.3 × 14.6 cm

17 Cyril Connolly, 1940
Pen and ink, 8⅜ × 5¾ in/21.3 × 14.6 cm

18 Boy on a bed, 1943
Pen and ink, 14¼ × 10 in/36 × 25.4 cm

21 David Gascoyne, 1942
Pen and ink, 4¾ × 7⅛ in/12 × 18 cm

23 Portrait of a girl, 1943
Brush and ink, 15½ × 12½ in/39.5 × 32 cm

84 Dead monkey, 1950
Pastel, 8⅜ × 14¼ in/21.2 × 36.2 cm
Collection the Museum of Modern Art,
New York, gift of Lincoln Kirstein

151 Francis Bacon, 1970
Pencil, 13 × 9⅜ in/33 × 23.8 cm

191 Drawing for naked figure, 1973
Brush and ink, 22 × 17¾ in/55.8 × 45.1 cm

202 Head of a girl, 1982
Charcoal, 15½ × 13½ in/39.5 × 34.3 cm

203 Girl with a monkey, 1978
Charcoal, 14⅛ × 20½ in/35.8 × 52 cm

PLATES

1 Frontispiece: Reflection –
   self portrait, 1981/82
   Oil on canvas, 12 × 10 in/30.5 × 25.4 cm

2 Three-legged horse, 1937
   Sculpture, sandstone, approx. 22 in/56 cm high

3 Still life with cactus and flower pots, 1939
   Oil on canvas, 24 × 20 in/61 × 50.8 cm

4 Woman in a multicoloured coat, 1939
   Oil on canvas, 22½ × 16 in/57.1 × 40.6 cm

5 Box of apples in Wales, 1939
   Oil on canvas, 23½ × 29½ in/59.7 × 74.9 cm

6 The refugees, 1941
   Oil on panel, 20 × 24 in/50.8 × 61 cm

7 Cedric Morris, 1940
   Oil on canvas, 12 × 10 in/30.5 × 25.4 cm

8 Landscape with birds, 1940
   Oil on panel, 15½ × 12¾ in/39.5 × 32.3 cm

9 The village boys, 1942
   Oil on canvas, 20 × 16 in/50.8 × 40.6 cm

10 Man in a striped shirt, 1942
    Oil on canvas, 16½ × 13¼ in/42 × 33.6 cm

11 Self portrait, 1939
    Oil on canvas, 12 × 9 in/30.5 × 23 cm

12 Tired boy, 1943
    Conté on buff paper,
    14 × 14 in/35.5 × 35.5 cm

13 Boy on a balcony, 1944
    Conté and crayon, heightened with white,
    21 × 14 in/53.3 × 35.5 cm

14 Juliet Moore asleep, 1943
    Conté and crayon on grey paper,
    13⅜ × 18¼ in/34 × 46.3 cm

15 Boy with a pigeon, 1944
    Conté and pencil heightened with white,
    19⅝ × 13 in/50 × 33 cm

16 Page from a sketchbook, 1941
    Ink and oil paint on paper,
    14⅝ × 9½ in/37.2 × 24.2 cm

17 Boy sitting with feet crossed, 1941
    Pen and ink, 14⅝ × 9½ in/37.2 × 24.1 cm

18 Man with a feather (self portrait), 1943
    Oil on canvas, 30 × 20 in/76.2 × 50.8 cm

19 Gerald Wilde, 1943
    Oil on panel, approx. 12 × 9 in/30.5 × 23 cm

20 Bottles in a recess, 1939
    Oil on canvas, 10¼ × 9½ in/26 × 24.1 cm

21 Man in a leather coat, 1943
Brush and ink, 15⅞ × 13 in/40.3 × 33 cm

22 Naval gunner, 1941
Pen and ink, 9 × 7 in/23 × 17.8 cm

23 Hospital ward, 1941
Oil on canvas, 10 × 14 in/25.4 × 35.5 cm

24 Dead monkey on a dish, 1944
Pen, ink and crayon, 8 × 13 in/20.3 × 33 cm

25 Still life with Chelsea buns, 1943
Oil on board, 15¾ × 20 in/40 × 50.8 cm
Collection the Museum of Art,
Carnegie Institute, Pittsburgh,
Pennsylvania
Gift of Mary C. Hazard in honour of
Leland Hazard (1893–1980) 1981

26 The painter's room, 1943
Oil on canvas, 24½ × 30 in/62.2 × 76.2 cm

27 Chicken in a bucket, 1944
Mixed media on paper,
15 × 15½ in/38 × 39.5 cm

28 Girl on the quay, 1941
Oil on canvas, 16 × 19¾ in/40.6 × 50.2 cm

29 Head of a woman, 1943
Conté heightened with white on buff paper,
18⅝ × 11⅞ in/47.3 × 30.1 cm

30 Cacti and stuffed bird, 1943
Pencil and crayon, 16⅛ × 21 in/41 × 53.3 cm

31 Dead bird, 1944
Conté and crayon, 7¼ × 5¼ in/18.4 × 13.3 cm

32 Woman with a tulip, 1945
Oil on panel, 9 × 5 in/23 × 12.7 cm

33 Quince on a blue table, 1943/44
Oil on canvas, 14½ × 23 in/36.8 × 58.4 cm

34 Woman with a daffodil, 1945
Oil on canvas, 9⅜ × 5⅜ in/24 × 14.5 cm
Collection the Museum of Modern Art,
New York

35 Loch Ness from Drumnadrochit, 1943
Pen and ink, 14⅝ × 17⅞ in/37.2 × 45.4 cm

36 Rabbit on a chair, 1944
Conté and chalk,
17¾ × 11¾ in/45 × 30 cm

37 Sea holly, 1944
Pen, ink and crayon,
16¾ × 20 in/42.5 × 50.8 cm

38 Chicken on a bamboo table, 1944
Pastel, conté and pencil,
dimensions unknown

39 Man with folded hands, 1944
Conté heightened with chalk,
$11\frac{5}{8} \times 17\frac{3}{4}$ in/29.5 × 45 cm

40 Dead heron, 1945
Oil on canvas, $19\frac{1}{4} \times 29\frac{1}{8}$ in/49 × 74 cm

41 Girl with roses, 1947/48
Oil on canvas, $41\frac{1}{2} \times 29\frac{3}{8}$ in/105.5 × 74.5 cm
Collection the British Council, London

42 Sleeping nude, 1950
Oil on canvas, 30 × 40 in/76.2 × 101.6 cm

43 Narcissus, 1947/48
Pen and ink, $8\frac{3}{4} \times 5\frac{3}{8}$ in/22.3 × 14.5 cm

44 Scotch thistle, 1944
Conté, pencil and crayon,
9 × 13 in/23 × 33 cm

45 Lemon sprig, 1946
Oil on board, $4\frac{1}{2} \times 7$ in/11.5 × 17.8 cm

46 Unripe tangerine, 1946
Oil on panel, $3\frac{1}{2} \times 3\frac{1}{2}$ in/9 × 9 cm

47 Daffodils and celery, 1946
Oil on canvas, 17 × 13 in/43.2 × 33 cm

48 Girl in a white dress, 1947
Conté, crayon and pastel on buff paper,
$22\frac{1}{2} \times 19$ in/57 × 48 cm

49 Girl with leaves, 1948
Conté and pastel on grey paper,
$18\frac{7}{8} \times 16\frac{1}{2}$ in/48 × 42 cm
Collection the Museum of Modern Art,
New York

50 Mother and baby, 1949
Ink on brown paper, $7\frac{1}{2} \times 4\frac{3}{4}$ in/19 × 12 cm

51 Ill in Paris, 1948
Etching, 5 × 7 in/12.7 × 17.8 cm

52 Girl in a dark jacket, 1947
Oil on panel, $18\frac{1}{2} \times 15$ in/47 × 38.1 cm

53 Christian Bérard, 1948
Black and white conté,
$16\frac{1}{8} \times 17\frac{1}{4}$ in/41 × 44 cm

54 Small Zimmerlinde, 1947
Oil on panel, dimensions unknown

55 Man at night (self portrait), 1947/48
Brush, pen and ink,
$20\frac{1}{4} \times 16\frac{3}{4}$ in/51.5 × 42.5 cm

56 Girl with a kitten, 1947
Oil on canvas, $15\frac{1}{2} \times 11\frac{5}{8}$ in/39.5 × 29.5 cm

57 Drawing from 'Flyda', 1947
Pen and ink, $5 \times 5\frac{1}{2}$ in/12.7 × 13.9 cm

58 Portrait of a girl, 1950
Oil on copper, $11\frac{5}{8} \times 9\frac{1}{4}$ in/29.5 × 23.5 cm

59 Girl with a white dog, 1951/52
Oil on canvas, 30 × 40 in/76.2 × 101.6 cm
Collection the Tate Gallery, London

60 Girl in a dark dress, 1951
Oil on canvas, 16 × 12 in/40.6 × 30.5 cm

61 Still life with aloe, 1949
Oil on panel, 8½ × 11¾ in/21.5 × 29.8 cm

62 Self portrait, 1952
Oil on canvas, 5 × 4 in/12.7 × 10 cm

63 Self portrait, 1949
Oil on canvas, 9⅞ × 6¾ in/25 × 17 cm

64 Francis Bacon, 1952
Oil on copper, 13 × 9⅜ in/33 × 23.8 cm
Collection the Tate Gallery, London

65 Detail of 66

66 Interior in Paddington, 1951
Oil on canvas, 60 × 45 in/152.4 × 114.3 cm
Collection the Walker Art Gallery,
Liverpool

67 A woman painter, 1954
Oil on canvas, 16 × 14 in/40.6 × 35.5 cm

68 Woman smiling, 1958/59
Oil on canvas, 28 × 22 in/71 × 55.8 cm

69 John Minton, 1952
Oil on canvas, 15¾ × 10 in/40 × 25.4 cm
Collection the Royal College of Art, London

70 Lincoln Kirstein, 1950
Oil on canvas, 19¾ × 15½ in/50.2 × 39.5 cm

71 Head of a woman, 1950
Oil on board, 10 × 8 in/25.4 × 20.3 cm

72 Girl in bed, 1952
Oil on canvas, 18 × 12 in/45.7 × 30.5 cm

73 Girl reading, 1952
Oil on copper, 8 × 6 in/20.3 × 15.2 cm

74 Girl in a green dress, 1953
Oil on canvas, 13¼ × 9½ in/33.5 × 24.2 cm
Collection the Arts Council of
Great Britain, London

75 Girl's head, 1954
Conté pencil, 13½ × 10 in/34.3 × 25.4 cm

76 A writer, 1955
Oil on canvas, 8¾ × 6¼ in/23 × 16 cm

77 Dead cock's head, 1952
Oil on canvas, 8 × 5⅛ in/20.3 × 13 cm
Collection the Arts Council of
Great Britain, London

78 Hotel bedroom, 1954
Oil on canvas, 36 × 24 in/91.5 × 61 cm
Collection the Beaverbrook Foundation,
Beaverbrook Art Gallery, Fredericton,
New Brunswick

79 A young painter, 1957/58
Oil on canvas, 16 × 15½ in/40.6 × 39.5 cm

80 Father and daughter, 1949
Oil on canvas, 36 × 18 in/91.5 × 45.7 cm

81 Girl by the sea, 1956
Oil on canvas, 9½ × 9¼ in/24 × 23.5 cm

82 Man in a headscarf, 1954
Oil on canvas, 12⅜ × 8⅝ in/31.5 × 22 cm

83 Boy's head, 1952
Oil on canvas, 8½ × 6¼ in/21.6 × 15.9 cm

84 Woman in a white shirt, 1956/57
Oil on canvas, 18 × 16 in/45.7 × 40.6 cm

85 Head of a boy, 1954
Oil on panel, 8 × 8 in/20.3 × 20.3 cm

86 Man with red hair, 1957
Oil on canvas, 15¾ × 13⅝ in/40 × 34.7 cm

87 Man smoking, 1956/58
Oil on canvas, 23 × 23 in/58 × 58 cm

88 Man in a mackintosh, 1957/58
Oil on canvas, 24 × 24 in/61 × 61 cm

89 Baby on a green sofa, 1961
Oil on canvas, 22 × 24½ in/55.8 × 62.2 cm

90 Pregnant girl, 1960/61
Oil on canvas, 36 × 28 in/91.5 × 71 cm

91 Ned, 1961
Oil on canvas, 7⅛ × 5½ in/18 × 14 cm

92 Woman's head with yellow background,
1963
Oil on canvas, 12½ × 9 in/31.8 × 23 cm
Rochdale Art Gallery

93 Red-haired man on a chair, 1962/63
Oil on canvas 36 × 36 in/91.5 × 91.5 cm

94 Figure with bare arms, 1961/62
Oil on canvas, 36 × 36 in/91.5 × 91.5 cm

95 Head on a green sofa, 1960/61
Oil on canvas, 36 × 36 in/91.5 × 91.5 cm

96 Naked child laughing, 1963
Oil on canvas, 13½ × 11 in/34 × 28 cm

97 Sleeping head, 1962
Oil on canvas, 26 × 20 in/66 × 50.8 cm

98 Man's head (self portrait I), 1963
Oil on canvas, 21 × 20 in/53.3 × 50.8 cm
Collection the Whitworth Art Gallery,
Manchester

99 Head, 1962
Oil on canvas, 20⅞ × 20⅞ in/53 × 53 cm

100 Man's head (self portrait III), 1963
Oil on canvas, 12 × 10 in/30.5 × 25.4 cm
Collection the National Portrait Gallery,
London

101 Man's head (self portrait II), 1963
Oil on canvas, 13 × 9½ in/33 × 24.1 cm

102 Cyclamen, 1964
Oil on canvas, 18 × 19⅜ in/45.7 × 49.2 cm

103, 104 Girl on a turkish sofa, 1966 (two states)
Oil on canvas, 10½ × 13¾ in/26.7 × 35 cm

105 Man in a blue shirt, 1965
Oil on canvas, 24 × 24 in/61 × 61 cm

106 John Deakin, 1963/64
Oil on canvas, 11⅞ × 9¾ in/30.2 × 24.8 cm

107 Reflection with two children (self portrait), 1965
Oil on canvas, 36 × 36 in/91.5 × 91.5 cm

108, 109 Two details of 107

110 Buttercups, 1968
Oil on canvas, 24 × 24 in/61 × 61 cm

111 A man and his daughter, 1963/64
Oil on canvas, 24 × 24 in/61 × 61 cm

112 A man, 1965
Oil on canvas, 18½ × 15½ in/47 × 39.5 cm

113 I miss you, 1968
Pen and ink, 13¼ × 9½ in/33.7 × 24.1 cm

114 Annabel, 1967
Oil on canvas, 13¾ × 10½ in/35 × 26.7 cm
Garman-Ryan Collection,
Walsall Museum and Art Gallery, Walsall

115 Annie reading, 1969
Oil on canvas, 7 × 10 in/17.8 × 25.4 cm

116 Small fern, 1967
Oil on canvas, 13½ × 11½ in/34.3 × 29.2 cm

117 Interior with plant, reflection listening
(self portrait), 1967/68
Oil on canvas, 48 × 48 in/121.8 × 121.8 cm

118 A filly, 1970
Oil on canvas, 7½ × 10½ in/19 × 26.6 cm

119 A filly, 1969
Mixed media on paper,
13½ × 9½ in/34.5 × 24 cm

120 Head of a woman, 1970
Oil on canvas, 9¼ × 7 in/23.2 × 17.8 cm
Collection the Gray Art Gallery and Museum,
Hartlepool

121 Night interior, 1969/70
Oil on canvas, 22 × 22 in/55.8 × 55.8 cm

122 Naked girl, 1966
Oil on canvas, 25 × 24 in/63.5 × 61 cm

123 Girl in a fur coat, 1967
Oil on canvas, 24 × 22 in/61 × 56 cm

124 Girl holding a towel, 1967
Oil on canvas, 19¼ × 19¼ in/48.8 × 48.8 cm

125 Naked girl asleep II, 1968
Oil on canvas, 22 × 22 in/55.8 × 55.8 cm

126 Naked girl asleep I, 1967
Oil on canvas, 24 × 24 in/61 × 61 cm

127 Woman in a fur coat, 1967/68
Oil on canvas, 23⅝ × 23⅝ in/60 × 60 cm

128 Factory in north London, 1972
Oil on canvas, 28 × 28 in/71 × 71 cm

129 Paddington interior, Harry Diamond, 1970
Oil on canvas, 28 × 28 in/71 × 71 cm
Collection the University of Liverpool

130 Small interior (self portrait), 1968/72
Oil on canvas, 8¾ × 10½ in/22.2 × 26.7 cm

131 Large interior, Paddington, 1968/69
Oil on canvas, 72 × 48 in/183 × 122 cm

132 Interior with hand mirror (self portrait),
1967
Oil on canvas, 10 × 7 in/25.5 × 17.8 cm

133 Wasteground, Paddington, 1970
Oil on canvas, 28 × 28 in/71 × 71 cm

134 Large interior, W.9, 1973
Oil on canvas, 36 × 36 in/91.5 × 91.5 cm

135 Annabel, 1972
Oil on canvas, 12½ × 9 in/31.7 × 22.8 cm

136 Detail of 137

137 Wasteground with houses, Paddington,
1970/72
Oil on canvas, 66 × 40 in/167.5 × 101.5 cm

138 Portrait fragment, 1971 (detail)
Oil on canvas, 24 × 24 in/61 × 61 cm

139 Naked portrait, 1972/73
Oil on canvas, 24 × 24 in/61 × 61 cm
Collection the Tate Gallery, London

140 Portrait of a woman, 1969
Oil on canvas, 27 × 23 in/68.5 × 58.4 cm

141 Portrait of a man, 1971/72
Oil on canvas, 27 × 27 in/68.5 × 68.5 cm

142 Last portrait, 1974/75
Oil on canvas, 24 × 24 in/61 × 61 cm

143 The painter's mother resting II, 1976/77
Oil on canvas, 10¼ × 16 in/26 × 40.6 cm

144 Girl with necklace, 1980
Charcoal, 12¾ × 9½ in/32.5 × 24.1 cm

145 Head of the big man, 1975
Oil on canvas, 16⅛ × 10⅝ in/41 × 27 cm

146 Head of a girl, 1975/76
Oil on canvas, 20 × 16 in/50.8 × 40.6 cm

147 The painter's father, 1970
Pencil, 9 × 6½ in/22.9 × 16.5 cm

148 The painter's mother III, 1972
Oil on canvas, 12¾ × 9¼ in/32.4 × 23.5 cm

149 The painter's mother II, 1972
Oil on canvas, 7 × 5½ in/17.8 × 14 cm

150 The painter's mother reading, 1975
Oil on canvas, 25¾ × 19¾ in/65.4 × 50.4 cm

151 Small naked portrait, 1973/74
Oil on canvas, 8⅝ × 10⅝ in/22 × 27 cm

152 Head on a brown blanket, 1972
Oil on canvas, 17½ × 10½ in/45.1 × 26.7 cm

153 Ali, 1974
Oil on canvas, 28 × 28 in/71.1 × 71.1 cm

154 Annie and Alice, 1975
Oil on canvas, 8⅞ × 10⅝ in/22.5 × 27 cm

155 Portrait of Ib, 1977/78
Oil on canvas, 16 × 12 in/40.6 × 30.5 cm
Collection the Cleveland Museum of Art,
Cleveland, Ohio

156 Detail of 157

157 The big man, 1976/77
Oil on canvas, 36 × 36 in/91.5 × 91.5 cm

158 Naked girl with egg, 1980/81
Oil on canvas, 29½ × 23⅜ in/75 × 60.5 cm
Collection the British Council, London

159 Naked portrait II, 1980/81
Oil on canvas, 35½ × 29½ in/90 × 75 cm

160 Two plants, 1977/80
Oil on canvas, 60½ × 48½ in/152.4 × 121.9 cm
Collection the Tate Gallery, London